JACK KEROUAC'S
AMERICAN JOURNEY

Also by Paul Maher Jr.

Kerouac:
His Life and Work

Empty Phantoms:
Interviews and Encounters with Jack Kerouac (editor)

JACK KEROUAC'S

AMERICAN JOURNEY

The Real-Life Odyssey of *On the Road*

PAUL MAHER JR.

THUNDER'S MOUTH PRESS
NEW YORK

JACK KEROUAC'S AMERICAN JOURNEY:
The Real-Life Odyssey of On the Road

Thunder's Mouth Press
An imprint of Avalon Publishing Group, Inc.
11 Cambridge Center
Cambridge, MA 02142

Library of Congress Cataloging-in-Publication Data is available.

ISBN-10: 1-56025-991-4
ISBN-13: 978-1-56025-991-6

9 8 7 6 5 4 3 2 1

Interior design by Maria E. Torres

Printed in the United States of America

Dedicated to
Paul Maher Sr.
1942–2004

Contents

If you be going the same road you will find me there, and I will tell you some curious things.

—Miguel de Cervantes, *Don Quixote*

Preface

I feel justified in explaining who Kerouac was before he became popularly known as the road-weary figure of the road. Above and beyond the sly putdown by critics of Kerouac as a "Neanderthal of the typewriter," he was both a powerful intellect and sensitive soul keen as he ever was to override the limitations of societal thinking and to instead embrace the kernel of life by peeling off its dying husk and devouring the life force wholly.

In April 1947, Jack Kerouac was preparing for his first long road trip, to California. In that same month and year,

Charles "Yardbird" Parker had returned to New York. The twenty-seven-year-old alto saxophonist was proving to be the most important musical soloist on the bebop scene. He had just recovered from a nervous breakdown, alcoholism, and heroin addiction, and was ready to reclaim his title as the decade's most formidable presence in jazz by forming a group consisting of Miles Davis, Max Roach, Duke Jordan, and Tommy Potter. Together they recorded some of bebop's most searing, original, and influential music. Parker's music was a string of unbroken notes going wherever he chose to take them. His philosophy was simple: "Music is your own experience, your own thoughts, your wisdom. If you don't live it, it won't come out of your horn. They teach you there's a boundary line to music. But, man, there's no boundary line to art." The same could be said about the writing of Jack Kerouac, who both adored Parker's music and recognized him as a serious musician on the same par as his other musical hero, Beethoven.

Jack Kerouac's approach to writing parallels Bird's musical insight. Kerouac wrote: "PROCEDURE. Time being of the essence in the purity of speech, sketching language is undisturbed flow from the mind of personal secret idea-words, *blowing* (as per jazz musician) on subject of image." For Kerouac, "blowing" about the road became a lifelong pursuit. The rigors of his travels enriched his pages while taking a toll on his mental health. He assessed himself in the early 1950s in a brutal, unforgiving, and candid self-portrait: "Hopper of freights, Skid Row habitué, railroad Buddhist, New England Modernist, 20th Century Storyteller, Crum, Krap, dope, divorcee, hype, type, sitter in window of life; idiot far from home; no wood in my stove, no potatoes in my field, no field; hepcat, howler, wailer, waiter in the line of time; lazy, washed-out, workless" (*Book of Sketches*, 398–99).

This bleak attitude was shored by a tenuous religious conviction that Christ and the Holy Spirit would ultimately lead the way toward his salvation. Catholicism and, sporadically, a fringe belief in Buddhism were his sole supports. Snaking between them was the long desolate road, both on page and in the reality of his life that he wandered alone, forlorn, searching for someone or something to replace the brother and father that he had lost in 1924 and 1946, respectively. Along that road lay his most famous and notorious novel titled *On the Road,* published in September 1957.

This book attempts to bring to life Kerouac's "road" years, from 1947 to 1951, and the novel that would reach true fruition with the creation of the legendary "scroll" version of *On the Road*. Understanding Kerouac's arduous physical trek and the thought processes he developed along the way provide a brand new appreciation for the legendary novel that continues to turn on generations to come.

On June 29, 1957, three months prior to *On the Road*'s publication, the *New York Times* printed a minor notice, perhaps the earliest related to *On the Road*, of a work by Jack Kerouac published in the avant-garde literary journal *New Directions*. This issue, the sixteenth, boasted sixty poems by Modernist poet William Carlos Williams; an essay by American novelist Henry Miller; a short play by Eric Bentley; a short story, "Color of Darkness," by James Purdy; as well as a selection from Kerouac's forthcoming novel, titled "A Billowy Trip in the World." It wasn't the first excerpt published from *On the Road*. The previous year, *The Paris Review* had printed "The Mexican Girl" and, in June 1957, an extended prose piece, "Neal and the Three Stooges," which had bounced in and out of different variants of *On the Road* before being finally inserted into his novel *Visions of Cody* (published posthumously in 1972).

Kerouac was exceptionally prolific through most of 1956 and into 1957. The months of hard literary labor produced a run of daring and exciting writing that demonstrated a fully mature voice and art. The result was literary experimentation that ranged from spiritual reflections to autobiographical fiction and playful poetry. In April 1956, intent on documenting his beliefs in and techniques of the practice of Buddhism, Kerouac wrote his one book that focused on the pure locus of distilled self-awareness, *The Scripture of the Golden Eternity*: "I was awakened to show the way," he wrote, "chosen to die in the degradation of life, because I am Mortal Golden Eternity."

Another work written during this time, more daring than

anything he had ever attempted before, was *Lucien Midnight,* named after Kerouac's Columbia friend Lucien Carr. The intention of the work was to evoke Carr's speech patterns (when Carr objected to the title, it was changed to *Old Angel Midnight*). During the fall of 1956, Kerouac completed a small novel called *Tristessa,* based upon his relationship with a prostitute junkie in Mexico City. Imbued throughout are his meditations on the human condition underpinned by the Buddhist credo that "All life is suffering." Toward its completion, he began another novel, *Desolation Angels,* drawing on his recent stint as a fire lookout in Washington State's Cascade Mountains. In early 1957, *On the Road* was accepted by Viking Press for its fall publication list that year.

1956 was also, as had been every year for the past nine, a year for traveling. In March, Kerouac hitchhiked to California from the home of his sister Caroline Blake (known as Nin) in Rocky Mount, North Carolina. After sharing a cabin with poet Gary Snyder in Marin County, California, he hitchhiked to Washington State for fire lookout training. From July through September, Kerouac was alone, for the most part, on Desolation Peak in the Cascade Mountains, where he compiled a series of ideas, sketches, poems, and personal comments in a series of notebooks. After fulfilling his obligations, he turned north toward Seattle before returning south to Mexico City.

Despite all of the writing he had done, *On the Road* was to be Kerouac's effort to "explain everything to everybody." He had been preparing, indirectly, to write it since his boyhood. Its theme conveyed the essence of a bygone America where the working classes struggled beneath the weight of the Great Depression. Those people who could not eke from society a meaningful living took to the rail and highways, propelling themselves across an equally despondent continent.

As early as 1943, in an autobiography written for a prospective employer in New York City, Kerouac depicted himself as a child of the working class. His Quebec-born, French-speaking father labored diligently as the owner of a printing press among the underpaid and exploited of Lowell, oftentimes mixing with the societal fringe of the vaudeville and theater circuit in the mill city. Leo Kerouac's weekly *Spotlight Print* inspired young Jean-Louis to write his own newspapers (among other pieces of writing). After completing high school, Kerouac received a football scholarship to Columbia University and, infused with Thomas Wolfe's relatively recent phone-directory-size novels, began roaming New York City and writing his own. Undeterred by likely failure, he sent out stories to top magazines, including *The New Yorker, Esquire,* and *Harper*'s without any success.

Kerouac sensed immensity in Wolfe, not just because of the size of his novels, but his daring approach toward capturing early-twentieth-century America. Wolfe, like Twain, dotted his novels with a vivid vernacular and explicit characterizations that gave his characters a genuine presence. In a later interview, Kerouac explained his fondness for Wolfe: "There's only one 20th century writer who could compare to Melville or Whitman—that's Thomas Wolfe. He's the only spirit of any dimension like real talkin' in the whole country since Melville. [Sinclair] Lewis was writing about a little bit of this, and Fitzgerald about a little bit of that. Hemingway a little bit of that. But Wolfe—put your ear to the ground at night in America and listen to thunderous hooves of the Blackfoot, the Indian. Hear the great railroad train. Ooh, he could hear everything when he put his ear to the ground" (from *Empty Phantoms: Interviews and Encounters with Jack Kerouac*).

Literature and an internal sense of rebellion was all that was needed to kick-start young Jack Kerouac's peripatetic inclinations. He wrote that at eighteen he discovered the "delight of rebellion," an attribute that helped him gain independence but was badly timed in an era of conformity and a sense of national identity that demanded far less individualism. He became "drunk" with his newfound self and, over the next two years, inspired by the ethnic writings of William Saroyan, his rebellion threatened to hurl him into chaos and darkness. Bouts of carousing in seedy bars and on street corners threatened his academic standing. Sampling marijuana for the first time, Kerouac had a taste of the drug that later conjured the mellowed-out overtones of his writing. In the city's shadows he followed the siren's call of the beckoning finger of a prostitute who had arisen "weeping on her bed of darkness."

Knowing full well that his destructive behavior could undermine his ambition to be an artist, but at the same time justifying his behavior so that he *could* be an artist, he attempted to unite the two: "I shortly gathered up my reins and began to direct those daring white steeds of rebellion into a more constructive direction—into a direction that was bound to be the beginning of ultimate, complete development & integration." Though his idealism may have been flawed, he set his sights on living purely by the advice of his spirit (despite the adverse effect it had on his family relations and college). He was a man, a "blind optimist," who wanted to "kick in an original manner." Kerouac's attempts to abide by this resulted in a reckless though merited existence.

The romanticism of the railroad caught his attention, and he filled pages with descriptions of smoke coiling above engines in the October air. Kerouac aligned the "real, the true America" with train tracks snaking west, disappearing around the bend and slipping into utter darkness: "My dawn is in the West!" Kerouac was hungry for new experience, as eager to devour a new mode of living as Thoreau had been to seize a woodchuck and eat it raw. He wrote on October 31, 1941: "Oh, yes, I am about to see life whole . . . man's travails, man plying his self-made civilization, man's decay, man's dignified despair and nobility. I am about to see it and smell it and eat it. It is going to be fine for me, I tell you. Fine for me, either way."

Ultimately Wolfe's road, exemplified by Eugene Gant's train ride along the American landscape, morphed into Kerouac's own open road. One day he left Columbia, unhappy over his sense of coaches Lou Little and Cliff Battle's favoritism of other players on the football team. How disillusioned Kerouac was is a matter of question; one rare photograph taken for the *New York Times* in 1942 reveals the distinctive movie-star profile of Kerouac, sitting ahead of the other team members, eagerly attentive to Little's explanation of gridiron strategy. The subheading of the news article reads "Coaches Work with Kerouac."

However, Kerouac had a plan and perhaps used the football excuse as a ploy to leave Columbia and pursue his own dreams. In his possession was a letter of introduction from a newspaper columnist to film director James Hogan of Republic Pictures. Clutching little else but a bag of clothes and some notebooks, Kerouac stepped onto a bus forever shifting the destiny of hard-living into his favor.

Though he started on the road to California, Kerouac somehow lost his nerve and ended up traveling south. He took on small jobs along the way, including working on the construction of the Pentagon in Washington, D.C. To save money to travel, he hopped freight trains from city to city, doing so for three months. However he feared the ramifications such rebellion would have on his parents who thought he was still in school. Dutifully, he returned home, resounding from the smart of familial obligation.

During the war years, when thousands of Kerouac's contemporaries were shipped overseas to fight, the young writer became discouraged by society's expectations, was crippled by his own indecision, and afflicted with an unconscious will to fail. He was drafted into the navy and discharged shortly thereafter for psychiatric reasons. (Later in his life, Kerouac bragged to bar patrons how he "tricked" the authorities into thinking he was "crazy.") His enlistment on various merchant marine vessels did more to fulfill his Jack London dreams than provide a solid sense of life direction.

After dropping out of Columbia University in 1942, sidestepping the more predictable path of academic success, a career, and a family, Kerouac's artistry began to become informed with a keen admiration for an America he sensed swiftly disappearing from the landscape. During and after the Second World War's chaos, fear, and uncertainty, he was hard at work, unfazed by the violence and ensuing gloom that dizzied the rest of the nation. He remained steadfast in his determination to cut a personal style from the multifaceted diamond of influences that sparkled before his eyes. Novels began piling up on his desk: *Merchant Mariner, The Sea Is My Brother,* and an early version of a novel he later published as *Vanity of Duluoz;* none truly satisfying his quest for vision. He read Twain, Saroyan, Wolfe, and Fyodor Dostoevsky, among others, in order to bring himself out of the pit of mediocrity he felt himself sinking in.

Lashing out toward his friend Allen Ginsberg in 1945 (perhaps out of frustration at knowing better but lacking the literary skills to prove it), a twenty-three-year-old Kerouac wrote accusingly: "[M]y art is more important to me than anything . . . None of that emotional egocentricity that you all wallow in, with your perpetual analysis of your sex-lives and such." Kerouac also knew that to succeed in his objective, he had to be selfish. "I dedicate myself to myself," he bluntly asserted. But Kerouac was also the epitome of paradox; his anger dissipating only one week later when he expressed an "indescribable need" to write Ginsberg to acknowledge that his own behavior was simply an "essential pose" of self-preservation. Closer to the truth was that he and Ginsberg shared a "common madness," dogged by a stubborn awareness of their potential. In the cage of their morality, it was necessary for them both to light the fireball of their passions, to *write,* to *document* their times accurately. In later years, Kerouac would tell Al Aronowitz of the *New York Post*, "Allen is the sweetest man in the world."

Back in New York City, Kerouac began writing anew, adopting a new vision for himself. He experimented with form and style—novellas and prose, snatches of poetry realized at length or abandoned mid-line—but he was never truly satisfied with the results. At the time of his father's death in 1946, Kerouac was outlining a full-length novel about the dynamics of a New England family and its dissolution following the Second World War.

In doing so, he steered himself into an entirely new mode of written expression. Drawing upon his life and utilizing his knack for poetic description, Kerouac found it quite easy to flesh the book out with not only a compelling narrative but also a spread of sibling characters, each possessing a facet of his own personality: brooder, wonderer, adventurer, thinker, and artist.

This mammoth work-in-progress, *The Town and the City,* began conventionally and ended by hinting in the direction he wished to go, though that was still largely to be determined by ulterior literary influences. This new work ultimately made it possible for him to capture unique American polarities: the profound spiritual loss following the Second World War and the ensuing quest for spiritual fulfillment; the legions of restless youth set adrift from parentless homes during the war years, and the stoic patriotism of the generation that lived through the Great Depression attempting to preserve the America they once knew, for better or for worse. There was the geography of those multiple Americas and their vanishing wilderness, the turbulent landscape of the soul; the longing for hope and despair's utter hopelessness, the world of the primitive *fellaheen* (a concept developed by philosopher Oswald Spengler) and those soulless moderns dueling to preserve their materialist way of life.

The novel, in all its deceptive simplicity, needed to absorb the most profound of Kerouac's cultural influences and apply it to modern America: Twain's Mississippi, Remington's West, Faulkner's South, Steinbeck's California, Thoreau's New England, and Saroyan's sociological reflections of ethnic heritage are some of the examples. Kerouac merged social classes on a broad palette to depict the human condition. He drew upon everything he accomplished in the past and, simultaneously, forgot it all in order to begin anew.

PART

1

CHAPTER ONE

BEFORE THE ROAD

Some Depression-era writers evoked restless characters. John Steinbeck's Okie migrants in *The Grapes of Wrath* (1940) demonstrated the duress of hard-working, religious people looking for honest work in the Golden Land of California. That search for redemption and identity, a plea for the restoration of family, homestead, and hope, was nonetheless an illusion. Those distant people in broken-down wagons and sputtering jalopies became a modern-day retelling of the Book of Exodus. William Faulkner's optimistic and angelic, yet barefoot and pregnant, Lena Grove, in *Light in August*

(1932), takes to the road searching for the father of her unborn child. Each character, like many others in novels at this time, evokes a pronounced sadness despite their disparate personalities (though they are all united by a common bond of loss).

Kerouac sought to express such themes in his own work. On August 23, 1948, he entered into his journal the first mention of this type of work, after a reading spell of Dostoevsky's short novel *Notes from the Underground* (1864), Joseph Conrad's novella *Heart of Darkness* (1902), and Mark Twain's *Tom Sawyer Abroad* (1894). Borrowing elements from his reading, Kerouac attempted a new style in the last chapter of *The Town and the City*, recognizing the fact that, at times, like Wolfe, he used "too many words." He justified this flaw because he knew that "true thoughts abound," a notion that "nullified" his wordiness. But it was time to "sharpen things" with a new novel: "I have another novel in mind—On the Road—which I keep thinking about: about two guys hitch-hiking to California in search of something they don't *really* find, and losing themselves on the road, and coming all the way back hopeful of something *else*" (journal entry, August 23, 1948). One way of constructing this bildungsroman would be to erase any notion of passing judgment, to capture the "human intensity of men" the "everpresent palpitation," the "pride to humility, back & forth, in the intenser neurotic sense, pride to humility, back and forth."The "nervous being" needed to be realized completely in order to distill a notion of "truth."

SELF-ULTIMACY

Kerouac drew up eleven rules for himself in an effort to define his "truths." He couldn't "waste" his time loving others, when after all he felt "better than they are"; he would justify "myself to myself" so that others could not perceive his "faults"; he would accept the inevitable truth of old age and death; the pride of greed, vice, and mortality; he would reject the participation in "life" as being beneath his dignity; he would admit the possibility of weakness without fear of being despised by others; he would surrender concern about the "bad[ness]" of others in favor of detecting it in himself; he would recognize that being "inured" to life's problems does not mean having solved them; he would avoid pride and favor in its stead aloofness; he would accept that admitting to truth is not to be vulnerable to "self-laceration"; and "I have struck out at the pride of others and then sat back and expected them to forgive me." Allen Ginsberg could certainly testify to that. Whenever Kerouac felt threatened by or envious of the poet's literary success, politics, or openly gay sexuality, Ginsberg would often be on the receiving end of Kerouac's paranoid wrath.

Recognizing self truth, Kerouac felt, would allow him to recognize it in others thus reaping empathy and understanding for the downtrodden. He would lift those above the "talking class," whom Kerouac deemed the "enemy of the country." "It is they who build New Yorks and Hollywoods, and flood our radios with inanity, and our papers and magazines with sterilized ideas . . . I mean the great 'Upper White Collar' class, the Commuters, the Whatnot, the people with snotty 'progressive' daughters six years old and sons who call their father 'daddy.'" Kerouac would alight on the heads of the underclass and lift them out of their woe and despair and with what he perceived to be an intact "truer" sense of spirituality.

Capturing this essence would be a feat, but one that could be accomplished by writing directly and honestly. Acknowledging Walt Whitman's "lesson of reception, nor preference nor / denial," Kerouac admired the broad beauty, sensitivity, and air of inclusion surmounting his poetry. With these touching and stirring words, Kerouac brought a perspective on his own sensibilities. Whitman celebrates in "Song of the Open Road":

> The black with his wooly head, the felon, the diseas'd the
> illiterate person, are not denied;
> The birth, the hasting after the physician, the beggar's tramp,
> the drunkard's stagger, the laughing party of
> mechanics,
> The escaped youth, the rich person's carriage, the fop, the
> eloping couple,
> The early market-man, the hearse, the moving of furniture
> into the town, the return back from the town,
> They pass, I also pass, any thing that passes, none can be
> interdited,
> None but are accepted, none but shall be dear to me.

Whitman in general and this poem in particular had a profound influence on Kerouac. His response to Whitman's identification with the oppressed possessed a "secret silent loathing and despair." Whitman's anger and depression, in the pre–Civil War period of 1837 to 1843 starkly parallels Kerouac's (and his fellow impoverished iconoclasts) post–World War II feeling that the people had somehow lost control of their country, especially so with the election of Dwight Eisenhower in 1953. Whitman reacted to racial bias, slavery, and the bewildering swamping of failed businesses and unemployment booming. Whitman's biographer David S. Reynolds writes that a "positive effect of the personal and public pain was that it turned Whitman toward reflection, creativity, and political sympathy with outcasts and losers, whose poetic champion he would one day become" (Reynolds, 53). Aligning himself with a similar task would not only be fitting, but also be an effective use of Kerouac's admiration for Whitman's persona and work. "Whitman," Kerouac pointed out a few months later, "has already pointed the way."

THE 1940S

The 1940s were a curious, yet century-defining span of years, a "bitter, gray" decade, as Beat poet Michael McClure described it. Americans, lifted out of the Great Depression, slowly regained their confidence as they rode an economic stallion of prosperity and stability. The Second World War created millions of jobs (although 8,120,000 were still unemployed in 1940). However, the fee for stable (and even disposable) income was paid with the lives of the nation's fathers and sons lost in foreign lands and seas. There were those soldiers rotting in the malarial jungles of Guadalcanal, some shot down on the deadly beaches of Normandy. Others of the maritime realm were sailors and merchant mariners floating like wan specters in the deep oceans of the world.

During World War II, women began filling the spots of their absent sons, fathers, and husbands, thus gaining an early foothold toward women's rights. Some were dressed in the current vogue, slacks, as they watched the ticking arms of the company clock marking off the hours of their men's absence.

America held its own in the battlefields of Europe and the South Pacific. Fervently it gripped patriotism's flag despite the stacking of the caskets in the holds of merchant ships crossing the great waters, berthing and unloading its fallen sons onto the city piers. For certain, victory had its price. Besides the many that had fallen, the nation was now $43 billion in debt. However, its victory assured a status as a world superpower. This, as the newspaper dailies made abundantly clear, was the prize of their war.

With conflicts seemingly resolved, the world settled back into its groove; peacetime offered prosperity and its strange bedfellow, conformity. The mid-1940s birthed a new form of adolescent, the juvenile delinquent. Especially in urban areas, youth crimes were the new statistic, an unfortunate by-product of the fractured nuclear family. Rebel youth inspired an explosion of films—*The Wild Ones, Rebel Without a Cause, Blackboard Jungle*—that dominated theater marquees.

By war's end, the United States has created its first nuclear weapon. Colossus, an enormous (and, by current standards, deficient and limited) computer, was built and programmed. Heroic Chuck Yeager made the world's first supersonic flight in 1947. In art, bebop granted jazz an introspection largely absent from the Big Band swing of Count Basie, Louis Armstrong, and Duke Ellington. The first indications of black consciousness were born from the precarious gains that had been achieved during World War II.

On the American plains and the rural farmlands of New England, the Northwest, and elsewhere, young men who had tasted wine from the vineyards of Beaujolais and bread baked from Spanish wheat and rye, were no longer satisfied on the acreage "in the family." The new GI Bill gave them an opportunity to attend colleges and universities, a level of education that until then, had only been available to the prosperous and athletic.

There were also those who championed the rights of minority races, who roamed among the hipsters and bohemians existing on society's outer fringes and, for better or for worse, were content to stay there. These came to be known as the Beat Generation.

OLD BULL LEE

October 1943 was the genesis of that gathering later recognized as the "beats." Kerouac said later in an interview that the beats, not yet using the word, "began forming a circle around Burroughs." William S. Burroughs, "Old Bull Lee" in the novel *On the Road,* was older than his associates (in both years and wisdom) and qualified as a teacher for Kerouac, because he spent all of his time "learning." Burroughs's self-education extended back to his youth in St. Louis in the '20s. Before he became an iconoclast, Burroughs wandered an endless maze of soul-searching. As an adolescent, Burroughs imagined himself a thief, a down-and-outer, and a writer thriving on the outermost fringes of decadence. On paper he scrawled pulp crime fiction rip-offs laced with narcotics and carnage.

As a teenager, Burroughs was admitted to the Los Alamos School for Boys in New Mexico, where, among other things, he learned to throw knives at targets and fire a rifle. However, beneath this thrill-seeking exterior lay a charnel house of remorse, guilt, desire, and frustration. He had a fondness for men but, knowing how society saw that, he purchased chloral hydrate, a sedative, from a pharmacist and swallowed a near-fatal dose. Students jeered at his love interests. Ultimately, with his parents' support, Burroughs dropped out. The school wrote, "His interest is in things morbid and abnormal, affects his sense of proportion in his work, making spotty and uneven results. His brain power, if rightly used, seems sufficient to get him into college, but there is doubt about his ability to direct himself." In another school in St. Louis, he directed himself sufficiently to gain admittance to Harvard University.

Harvard was a WASP-ish school and Burroughs, predictably, did not fit in. After graduation, his parents gave him a ticket to Europe. In Vienna, he attempted to study medicine while creeping along the razor's edge of an illicit lifestyle. However, in 1937, the Nazi party was installed in the government and Burroughs, uncomfortable, withdrew from the college and took with him a bride. She was a thirty-five-year-old Jewish woman who latched onto the young American purely for a marriage of convenience. In New York, they went their separate ways. Burroughs would divorce her years later in Mexico in the company of his second common-law wife, Joan Adams.

Burroughs once again returned to school, now focusing his studies on psychoanalysis and anthropology. By late 1939, he became involved with a twenty-five-year-old man who was part office boy and part hustler. Burroughs's sexual proclivities still tortured him. In a fit of desperation, he took a shiny pair of poultry shears, regained his manic composure before a vanity mirror, and snipped the tip of his little finger off his left hand. He felt euphoric, freed of the stigma of sexual deviance. His analyst thought otherwise and recommended a stint at Bellevue Hospital.

Upon release, Burroughs went to Chicago's seamy North Side, where he met Herbert Huncke, another hustler and petty thief involved in narcotics. Taking Burroughs's arm, Huncke gave him a grand tour of the criminal underworld Burroughs had fantasized about often as a teenager. It was through Huncke, "the greatest storyteller I've ever known," that he first learned of the word "beat" in 1948. "We learned the word from him. To me it meant being poor," Kerouac explained to Al Aronowitz in 1959, "like sleeping in the subways, like Huncke used to do, and yet being illuminated and having illuminated ideas about apocalypse and all that." Burroughs, another source of apocalyptic "illuminated ideas" was a guru of a sort to both Huncke, Kerouac, and later, legions of dedicated readers.

In the fall of 1942, Burroughs met Lucien Carr and David Kammerer, who spent some time on the North Side before returning to New York City. In the spring of 1943, he willingly followed them.

CARLO MARX

The slight, bookish Allen Ginsberg (Carlo Marx in *On the Road*) was born on June 2, 1926, to a Socialist father, Louis Ginsberg, and a Communist mother, Naomi. Naomi unintentionally endowed her son with empathy toward the disadvantaged, a lifelong trait he poignantly expressed to strangers, friends, and family alike. Naomi had been displaying symptoms of schizophrenia since 1919 and entered a sanitarium when Allen was three. Habitually walking around the house nude in front of her children while preaching communism, she was convinced that her husband was trying to poison her. She began hearing voices, thought insects were trying to enter her body through her ears, and feared being assassinated.

Allen fared little better. Easily frightened by shadows on his bedroom wall, he conjured up the mystical figure of the Shrouded Stranger, a concept Kerouac borrowed for *On the Road.* At the age of eleven, Ginsberg expressed a need for sexual contact with his family members in his diary. At the age of sixteen, he consulted a manual to answer the question, "Am I a homosexual?" It was, he thought, the catalyst for self-examination.

Allen Ginsberg knew that he wanted to labor for the welfare of the working class, a theme that would be dotted throughout his poetry and activities for the rest of his life. In the fall of 1943, the seventeen-year-old Ginsberg entered Columbia University, supported by a scholarship and university stipend. Though his motives for going were more than academic, he ultimately endeared himself to the English department. By the time he had completed his first semester, Ginsberg had found a new source of knowledge—William S. Burroughs.

BREAKING AWAY

Kerouac met Burroughs in February 1944 and Allen Ginsberg later that spring. Their mutual interests in literature, philosophy, and writing unified the beat collective. They met in the apartment of Joan Vollmer Adams at 421 West 118th Street. Hers was an unassuming yellow-brick six-floor building. Her apartment was so vast that she could take in boarders in her four-bedroom apartment. It was expensive enough that she needed help to pay rent, the first being Hal Chase (Chad King in *On the Road*), a Columbia student originally from Denver, Colorado.

In 1946, Kerouac retreated from his friends to the Ozone Park home he shared with his parents. He had married Edie Parker, a woman he had met at Columbia. However, unable to maintain a solid relationship with a woman, Kerouac enlisted in the merchant marine. He felt his time at sea absolved him of all the guilt that bogged him down at home: "just a few hours after all that junk of bars, fighting, streets, subways, boom, there I am standing by whipping shrouds and snapping lines in the Atlantic Ocean in the night off New Jersey [. . .] everything is washed away by the sea."

Harassment by a fellow sailor and his fondness for a woman in the city caused Kerouac to impulsively jump ship and go into hiding with Allen in Manhattan, unbeknownst to his wife and parents. His intentions, at this point, were to commence writing anew, intoxicated by a heady brew of literary and philosophical influences. Kerouac said later that he burned most of what he had written at this point, a claim that does not concur with his vast extant archive, which holds much of what he had written in his youth.

Consumed with the notion of being a life-changing artist, Kerouac clung to the idea that attaining such a lofty goal was not only possible, but permissible. The surrealistic images of Jean Cocteau's French film *The Blood of a Poet* (1930) drove home the point that the written word could still retain its power even matched with random visual images and without a semblance of a linear narrative.

"[I]t was a year of low, evil decadence," marked by his use of "bennies," an amphetamine. He used the drug tentatively at first, but when he found that he could write on it, he indulged constantly, to the detriment of his health. His self-description in *Vanity of Duluoz* is telling; a "pale skin-and-bones" visage that concerned his ailing father who saw his gaunt distant son in company of the worst associates, Ginsberg and Burroughs.

The Beat circle ensconced in Joan Vollmer's apartment was complete by spring 1946. In a narcotic haze, they shared passages from books by Celine, Dostoevsky, Baudelaire, and Spengler. Each burdened with dysfunctional baggage, they could have quoted Baudelaire—"I have felt the winds of the wings of madness"—and meant it. Depraved lifestyle and depraved thoughts merged, leaving Kerouac with no recourse other than to stand back and objectify it the best he could.

Leo Kerouac, now suffering from Banti's syndrome, a chronic disease of the spleen, was permanently bedridden and unable to earn an income. The disease, afflicting any one of the networks of veins from the spleen to the heart, was debilitating. Kerouac alludes to Banti's and to cancer of the spleen, or both, as the final terminating agent of Leo's life.

Kerouac's health was a concern, too. A bout of thrombophlebitis (which may be the "serious illness" that Sal Paradise alludes to in the opening sentences of *On the Road*), struck him one day while crossing the Brooklyn Bridge with Allen Ginsberg. He collapsed in agony onto the ground. Admitted to a hospital in Queens, the temporary halt to his frantic activities gave him time to meditate upon what he had accomplished, or not accomplished, thus far: "I began to get a new vision of my own of a truer darkness which just overshadowed all this overlaid mental garbage of 'existentialism' and 'hipsterism' and 'bourgeois decadence' and whatever names you want to give it." This, not the death of his father, was the turning point in his young life, the seismic shift of his life objectives.

Kerouac's convalescence brought him back home where he watched helplessly as his father's once-bulky frame wasted away to nothing. Despondent at his feeling of utter helplessness (his mother, Gabrielle, was the sole breadwinner now, skiving shoes at a shoe factory in Brooklyn), he outlined a new novel, *The Town and the City.* The brunt of it would detail the Martin family, living in their rural hometown, "Galloway," based on Kerouac's own hometown, Lowell. The "city" half of the book would take place in New York City.

On May 17, 1946, Leo Kerouac died in his chair. The

stunned son watched some Brooklyn undertakers place him into a casket and a hearse, taking him back to his hometown of Nashua, New Hampshire. Mother and son followed the body until it was lowered into an unmarked plot next to the tomb of Gerard, the ghostly brother who was for Kerouac and his mother the barometer of moral and religious virtue.

At Leo's death, Kerouac promised that he would protect and care for his mother, the usual duty of the "man of the family." Gabrielle continued working at the factory while he fumbled with the unwanted stamp of "responsibility" thrust upon him. He felt a tweak of Catholic guilt, but also the privilege of the artist. "I am a hoodlum and a saint," he confided in his 1947 journal. "The experience of life is a regular series of deflections that finally results in a circle of despair." He began thinking of leaving behind his Manhattan friends and hunkering down in Ozone Park to write his novel.

FORGING A NEW PATH

The first efforts at *On the Road* were born in isolation and introspection. In 1945, Kerouac had experimented with its style in a novella, *Orpheus Emerged,* with its "organic" prose; and in *The Haunted Life,* a highly stylized prose piece. The former he found to be "particular" and precise; the latter, more "lyrical." His task, it seemed, was to combine the two.

Underneath the violent beat of his artistic impulses was the realization that he had limitations as a writer. He would have to keep on writing, stockpiling page after page, ideas upon ideas, even if it meant discarding a good portion of the writing. However, he conceived the idea of creating an experimental novel in which he could use all of the numerous facets of his imagination and, beneath it all, utilize "actual experience" as a "screen" to make the "shadows dance." This, he knew, would require an inventiveness of fierce ambition. Art had curative powers. It had saved him after he was discharged, for psychiatric reasons, from the United States Navy and given him buoyancy while others sank into despair. Though his will was impaired by anxiety and nervousness, it was necessary to overcome the impediment and establish a solid precedent for living. Living meant art, and all else would come behind it.

Infused with the power of Shostakovich's Fifth Symphony, by the mysterious Kafka, and by Joyce's profuse experimentation in *Finnegans Wake,* Kerouac wrestled with characters his imagination would flesh into perfection, only to have them later dissolve into muddled anonymity. From the exile in his imagination, cities rose, faces swam from fog banks into identity, and faraway places became familiar. Yet there was also maddening frustration; living in two worlds, reality and imagination, meant that the trip from one to the other was far too vast to allow him to "retain a momentary perspective of either."

All of the writers that he read—Dostoevsky, Wolfe, Joyce, and André Gide, for example—had mastered the form that seemed to elude Kerouac. There was something to be said for writing with clarity and conciseness. In Gide's *The Counterfeiters,* a novel about Parisian life before World War I, the author's skill at interconnecting characters, coupled with the underlying morality, caused Kerouac much consternation. He found the work deliberately concise however; its overall clarity left him cold, and he felt it left no mark upon him as a reader.

He turned to other works, including Aldous Huxley's *Point Counter-Point,* which avoided Gide's shortcomings (as he perceived them), especially in its expression of overall awareness. Awareness, after all, was what he was after in his own work. Ultimately, he insisted that "life is holy," that it is "always" necessary to preserve mutual reverence, and it was the only truth. It is *this* truth that he deemed necessary to his work. He was pursuing it in another work he had been laboring over since 1944. *Michael Daoulas, Vanity of Duluoz* had grown to fifty-two pages before it stopped. The problem was how to create an ending; it needed *awareness, particulars,* and *organic unity,* the same issues he experienced with the others. He had amassed thirty pages of notes on characters, divided the work into sections, and created a dramatic arc, but that stubborn mule called *style* forestalled its completion.

One plan would be to use his real life as creative fodder. It was *him,* this *life* that he called *his,* that had to be used. From it he extracted a mind-scattered Benzedrine weekend when the world seemed to scatter off into haphazard dashes. The main character, Michael Daoulas, was left alone in the oppressive darkness confronted only by a keen sense of human awareness, divorced from a sense of identity, while his wife slept obliviously next to him. Daoulas knew that he could never love her, that he *cannot* love her, just as Kerouac could not love Edie Parker the way she wanted. Life is passionately unified with death; the "piling up" of "artistry," the clashing of dualisms, at once contradictory, endearing, and poised between beauty and horror. He could *see* it, he could *feel* it, but he could not *write* it.

At this time, Kerouac was in correspondence with Henri Cru (Remi Boncouer in *On the Road*), a classmate at Horace Mann Prep school, who had remained a friend. Cru was one year older than him and, like Kerouac, was also a Massachusetts native. Cru had introduced him to Edie Parker two years before they married in a Bronx jail but, after their nuptials, Cru was baffled, hurt by, and resentful of their marriage. Now Cru, who had become a merchant seaman, suggested that Kerouac once again take to sea. It would be a convenient escape, with a deceptive aura of "responsibility"—gainful employment without the drudgery of walking to work every day, lunchbox in hand. "It is beneath my dignity to participate in life," Kerouac wrote. Furthermore, the pathetic sight of his mother ("bowlegged in my dreams") leaving the apartment in the morning, as he commonly slept in from a long night of reading and writing, was too much to take. His sister Nin also incessantly badgered her brother, making him feel nothing more than an opportunistic loafer.

The new book was his ace in the hole from which he gambled it would offer up a "living." He yearned to earn enough from the advance to live on and buy some land, perhaps a farm and from its proceeds travel the world. In June 1947, Kerouac asked himself the question, "Why do I want to write this?" What pleasure did it bring? What joy? His goals were too broad, too vague, extending far beyond the reach of his capabilities. "I wish I could write from the point of view of one hero instead of giving everyone in the story his due value." With that conflict, the manuscript grew and grew until it might resemble nothing more to shallow critics than a Thomas Wolfe knock-off. Undermining this effort was another dichotomy anchored in the philosophies of the two Russian masters, Tolstoy and Dostoevsky. Kerouac's worldview perfectly, if coincidentally, embodied the idealisms of the two writers.

Tolstoy's collection, called "moral essays" in his journal, is titled *The Kingdom of God Is Within You*. In Kerouac's opinion, it was a book by a man self-conscious of the world's view of him after a glowing career crowned by such masterworks as *War and Peace* and *Anna Karenina*. Kerouac's impression was colored by his fondness for Dostoevsky's *The Brothers Karamazov,* whose peasantry seemed to him far more genuine than the wealthy count who stooped to their level only later in his life. "Dostoevsky never *had* to retire to morality, he was always it, and everything else also." Kerouac referred to Tolstoy's *Kingdom* again and again in his last decade, famously paraphrasing its "hourglass" reference during his appearance on William F. Buckley Jr.'s *Firing Line* broadcast in 1968.

In sum, the 1940s were a stepping stone for Kerouac. The period offered opportunity, new friends, a formative writing experience and, at the latter reach of the decade, the formidable road.

CHAPTER TWO

First Trip on the Road, June 1947–October 1947

DEAN MORIARTY

After working on a Colorado ranch, twenty-year-old Neal Cassady drove east to New York City with his new bride, LuAnne Henderson. He had seen her in a Denver drugstore when she was fifteen years old and, as the myth goes, immediately vowed to his friends to marry her. Not long after, on August 1, 1946, he did just that. Cassady had been paroled from the Colorado State Reformatory only the year before, where he had been sent for car theft.

In October 1946, Cassady and LuAnne reached Manhattan. They walked along Fiftieth Street, their mission to find Hal Chase, the Denver native who was then living near Columbia University. They found him at a campus bar. In a neighboring booth was Allen Ginsberg, and the two met for the first time, uneventfully. Ginsberg made LuAnne feel uncomfortable about her name, which he found "strange." Though Ginsberg could not help them with a place to live, they eventually made do with a cold-water flat in Spanish Harlem.

Cassady then met Jack Kerouac.

It wasn't an earth-shattering occasion. Kerouac never mentions the meeting, even offhandedly, in his journal. Kerouac was always meeting people in Manhattan at parties, in bars, diners, or nightclubs, so that the likelihood is that Cassady, on their first meeting, made little impression upon Kerouac. However, the event assumes a prominent status in Kerouac's posthumous novel, *Visions of Cody* (after Kerouac could truly then appreciate the heroic nature of the novel's subject).

In *Visions of Cody*, Kerouac knocks on the door of the Spanish Harlem flat accompanied by Hal Chase and Ed White (Tim Gray in *On the Road*). Neal Cassady answered, stark naked, with a rumpled LuAnne leaping to straighten her dress and fix her hair. Chase had described Cassady to Kerouac and Ginsberg as a "mad genius of jails and raw power" as well as a "Nietzchean hero of the pure snowy wild West." He had read Schopenhauer in reform school, and one of his chief attractions for girls was his "big huge crown" (VOC,

338). (Hal Chase's attraction to Cassady extended also to Kerouac, who described one night in a Boston hotel of waking up to find Chase's hand on the crotch of his pants.) In homoerotic tones in *Visions of Cody,* Kerouac noted Cassady's perfect build, his blue eyes, and his resemblance to the western movie and singing star Gene Autry. Kerouac was amazed by his beauty.

Alternately, Kerouac's first impression was how "dishonest-looking" Cassady was. His handsome looks betrayed the numerous cars he had stolen and the nights in jail. His countenance brought to mind the French Canadian men of Lowell, Massachusetts, who were "real tough, sometimes were boxers, or hung around rings, gyms, garages, porches in the afternoon" (VOC, 339). They were the guys who got the best-looking girls and escorted them home after a sweaty night by the dump of the Merrimack River, tossing their used condoms as they walked away. That evening of their first encounter, Kerouac slept in a chair. Cassady and LuAnne slept clothed on the couch. The others had staggered off to their respective homes after a long night of partying.

The next morning, Kerouac woke up, lit a cigarette, and watched Spanish Harlem come to life outside the window. Cassady barked orders to LuAnne. She swept the floor, cooked breakfast, and let Cassady and Kerouac dominate the proceedings. Kerouac lusted after LuAnne and, with Cassady's consent, he was able to bed her. Sometimes he did so in Ozone Park, presumably when the prudish Gabrielle was away. Jack and Neal book-ended a naked LuAnne on the same bed Leo Kerouac died in: "therefore giving that bed some life to renew it and give it direction in the empty void (and sagged in the middle from a once-mighty weight); lay stiff as an iron board at or upon his edge of the bed, Joanna [pseudonym for LuAnne] sunk hot in the middle and smiling and a little embarrassed and thinking of something else" (VOC, 341).

According to Cassady, who now considered Kerouac a "close friend," they all went to a Ninth Street apartment building to buy some pot on January 10, 1947. The door opened to a woman named Vicki, and Ginsberg. Ginsberg had found Vicki as "unattached and as attractive as any woman I know," but was too unnerved to be more than a friend. She had been among the circle consisting of Ginsberg, Kerouac, Lucien Carr, John Kingsland, and Celine Young. Her "meal ticket," in the words of Cassady, who quoted Kerouac in an unpublished writing fragment, was a man named Norman who was "hung up on his analyst" and the rigors of his "Reichian-Analysis." Besides drugs, Vicki had issues with her "nympho tendencies," something Kerouac had taken advantage of in the not-too-distant past.

Later, when Cassady's caustic insensitivities had been overtaken by the mythical status that Kerouac foisted upon him, the latter provided a revisionist outlook for his old friend in an interview with Al Aronowitz in 1959: "Neal is more like Dostoevsky than anybody else I know. He looks like Dostoevsky, he gambles like Dostoevsky, he regards sex like Dostoevsky, he writes like Dostoevsky. I got my rhythm from Neal. Neal was a great pool-room saint. Neal Cassady and I love each other greatly." Ironically, Cassady was no longer that close to him at the time. He'd been imprisoned in San Quentin since 1958, sentenced to five years for a marijuana drug bust (he only served two).

The Cassadys moved to Bayonne, New Jersey. On January 14, 1948, LuAnne, walking home from her bakery job, got lost in a snowstorm that obscured any recognizable landmarks. Already angered by her husband's frequent absences and lack of attention toward her, she was even more incensed when she came home to an empty house. Fed up, LuAnne fled home to her mother in Colorado. Cassady, for all intents and purposes, was all Ginsberg's now, at least sexually, for the next six weeks.

CARLO MEETS DEAN

Though Ginsberg hadn't the courage to act on his homosexual urges (he had only recently outed himself to Lucien Carr and was serenely comforted by Kerouac's gentle if unbinding acceptance), he felt confident enough with the new stranger to begin a sexual relationship shortly after their second meeting. One night, Ginsberg and Kerouac walked Cassady back to Spanish Harlem. The late hours gave cause for them to stay at Cassady's apartment, where there were two beds available. Kerouac slept in a double bed with Bob Malkin, the official tenant of the flat. Ginsberg and Cassady shared the other. There they consummated their mutual lust for one another.

By January 21, Ginsberg had noted the "sexual drama" he endured with Cassady the previous weekend and was now willing to "approach Neal and propose to him that we live together for a season, short or long as it may be." He was aware that he had little to offer the dynamic and charismatic Cassady except his "intellectual polish, learning, subtlety of thought." Cassady had made a point of bringing up the idea that he now wanted to attend Columbia, join the football team, and pursue academics. However, his formal education was distinctly lacking, and the two feet of Harvard Classics he claimed to have consumed while at the reformatory would not be counted. Strolling Morningside Heights, he asked Kerouac to see if he and Hal Chase could find a way to get him enrolled as an undergraduate.

By February 23, Ginsberg was graphically dreaming up "sexual positions" that he would find pleasing to himself as practiced on Cassady: "It is unfortunate that as yet I am unable to woo him with speech, but, in bed, merely discuss things with earnestness." Ginsberg, his head spinning with Alexander Pope, Andrew Marvell, Samuel Johnson, and Charles Baudelaire, dispensed with the intellectual small-talk, and focused on the real benefits of the situation at hand: "try him laying me again; try breast to breast position.

Try 69 again, coming both at once. Try sitting on his chest making him blow me." All of these ideas, according to Cassady's second wife, Carolyn, would have repulsed Cassady tremendously.

Two weeks later, Ginsberg had finally relayed his smarts to a willing and accessible Cassady, who he sensed had a "special way of thought." He was open to experience, he was pensive, he brooded much as Kerouac did when troubled or inspired. Ginsberg, who was still attempting to understand himself, had far worse luck with Cassady. His impulsive spirit made him undependable. Though Kerouac could be as cerebral as Ginsberg, he wasn't outwardly so, preferring to register his thoughts in writing. Ginsberg knew that Cassady dug Kerouac because, though he was an intellectual, it wasn't something he wore on his sleeve. "He and Jack go out and experience together . . . ," Ginsberg noted in his journal on March 2, 1947. Ginsberg knew, of course, how easy it was to talk to Kerouac: "with Jack, I can let myself go." Cassady's letting go fed Kerouac's inspiration and he mined that vein for all that it was worth. It was a relationship that Ginsberg felt Kerouac would never have with him, for he felt that he thought of him as "insignificant" (BMA, 180–2).

Ginsberg's reason for his moroseness was displayed in a lengthy March 2 journal entry. Cassady's departure via Greyhound bus was scheduled for the next day. Freshly garbed in a twelve-dollar pinstripe suit, a stolen overcoat (a gift from Ginsberg, who obtained it from the petty thief William

Garver, who stole coats from restaurants and sold them to pawn shops to feed his heroin habit), and a typewriter that might have been stolen or bought, Cassady boarded a Thirty-fourth Street bus for the initial leg of his journey back to Denver. Ginsberg would follow him in a few weeks.

Kerouac did not hear from Cassady until some days later. In a letter, Cassady exhibited another side of himself, not of the confident cocksman but of a man attempting to express himself with a "continuous chain of undisciplined thought." He wrote in fast, terse sentences detailing an attempted seduction of two women on his bus. Cassady spared Kerouac of any excessive description, but it was still a startling change for Kerouac, who up to now had been used to a snide cattiness and a lot of intellectual swordplay from his New York friends. The letter was nicknamed the "Great Sex Letter"; its existence later became a testament to the mystery of Neal Cassady and the mythic West that seemed to promise *something*. For the record, of the two potential Cassady conquests, one proved to be a failure (because of a bothersome sister waiting for her at a bus station) and the second a successful score.

MY BIG HALF-MANUSCRIPT

Freed of the Cassady distraction, Kerouac renewed his vigor to write his novel. For a while, he had relations with a woman named Beverly Burford (formerly a love interest of Ed White's). Their fondness for one another usually involved sharing a bottle of wine and talking until dawn. However, she was peripheral to Kerouac's life at the moment, for he was in the midst of a feverish spell of creativity. Typing and retyping his chapters, Kerouac recorded his daily tally into his journal: 2,000 words, 1,800 words, 1,500, 1,000, 950. Each day fluctuated, but by June 16 he disclosed that he had accomplished all "380,000—odd words of it."

Kerouac's sole wish was to gain enough financial freedom with his book to "earn a living" and to free his mother from her servitude at the shoe factory (and it was damned hard work even if the average Joe could see no merit in it). He had no patience for the American public, which had recently developed a taste for streamlined easy-to-digest novels instead of more meaty tomes like Thomas Wolfe. He was not alone in his ambition. In 1947 John Steinbeck began framing his next novel, the ambitious and lengthy *East of Eden,* to be published in September 1952.

Kerouac's confidence waxed and waned. Some days were a blazing display of ambition outpaced by imagination. Swallowing Benzedrine to give him the edge he needed, he sweated out a few thousand words and slept it off until late in the morning the next day. Part of his problem, he realized, was his overextended generosity toward his characters. If he overcame his temptation to make all of his characters "heroes," things would go faster.

Morality was another bump in the road. The attempt to saddle the bucking steer of his moral fiber was a difficult task;

Kerouac again looked to Leo Tolstoy for answers, but *The Kingdom of God Is Within You* did not give him the answer he was seeking: "I writhed and wrestled to the conclusion that morality, moral concept, is a form of melancholy." Morality, he told himself was "not for me." Instead, he resorted to the *other* Russian who had been his constant mainstay since starting classes at Columbia. Informally he called him "Dusty." Fyodor Dostoevsky's *The Brothers Karamazov* gave Kerouac a collection of characters he could identify with. For didn't each Karamazov posses certain character traits that composed the synthesis of Jack Kerouac? There was the sensuous Dmitri, fond of copious drink and loose women, celebratory and eager for experience; Ivan, the atheistic intellectual (though Kerouac was no atheist, he was anticlerical like his father and questioned the church's authority over its flock); and Aloysha, the young, handsome, thoughtful son of a contrastingly gentle strain. Kerouac identified with each and, perhaps, bled from Dostoevsky's greatest work the idea to create several brothers in *The Town and the City* of contrasting personalities. "Dostoevsky's wisdom is the highest wisdom in the world, because it is not only Christ's wisdom, but a Karamazov Christ of lust and glees." This comment, in reference to the "Grand Inquisitor" chapter, may be the greatest indication of Kerouac's disenchantment with the church. God and Christ were very real entities in Kerouac's spiritual world, each governing the dark morass of his brooding hours.

Ivan's parable, told to Aloysha, concerns the appearance of Christ in Seville during the Spanish Inquisition. He begins to perform miracles, which win him the adoration of the crowd. However, he is arrested by officials and brought to a jail cell. The Grand Inquisitor visits Christ in his cell. He is, the Inquisitor explains, no longer needed. Furthermore, the three temptations of Satan, which Christ rejected to assure humanity's freedom from sin, is equally problematic.

By equipping mankind with the freedom to choose, Christ has bestowed upon them something they cannot handle. This, by happenstance, dooms the weaker portion of humanity to eternal suffering. The teachings of Christ, in Kerouac's words, offer a "turning-to, a facing-up, a confrontation and a *confoundment* of the terrible enigma of human life" (WW, 15). Before Christ offered the parables to the eager masses, men and women thought "long dark silent thoughts." In the constant paradoxical efforts of existence lie the enigma that "confounds the senses" (WW, 16). It is the "riddle of life" that presents a "moral proposition."

Humanity's acceptance or denial of this message in turn offers redemption or doom. Like such works as Melville's *Moby Dick* and Wolfe's *You Can't Go Home Again, The Brothers Karamazov* serves up such conundrums to the reader. Kerouac wished to do the same. He had begun reading the New Testament with a fervor previously absent from his life. Devotion to the Word, or at least a missionary zeal to abide by its principles, was admirable except, as Kerouac noted, he had a family that expected, at some point, to have him contribute toward expenditures. "Can I go about in camel's hair, and leathern gird, and subsist on locust and wild honey?" he wondered in the pages of his journal. Nevertheless, he prayed deeply and with a solid will: "Oh I am not humble / Give me this last gift, God, and I will / be humble, I will owe You humbleness, / but only give me the gift."

Kerouac's work-in-progress had finally found its unifying threads: the nuclear family, a strong setting, and a plot. Gathering various examples of families he knew of (including his own), splitting up the personalities and psyches of his own family and the Karamazovs among the Martin brothers, Kerouac drew upon memory, imagination, and soul-searching.

Earlier, he had made more modest, though no less ambitious, attempts to distill his brainstorms into short prose pieces, stories, plays, and essays. During October 1944, his "Dialogues in Introspection" discussed morality, sin, and society in an eight-page dialogue. That same month he also wrote "The Dark Corridor," several pages of philosophy fused with mysticism. "The Repertoire of Modern Idea" was an attempt to analyze modern philosophy. His ideas would run their erratic course for three to ten pages before retiring, or he would abruptly move to another topic.

On November 15, 1944, he was terse and blunt, disgusted by art. Similar sentiments are sprinkled throughout the pages of his journal during forays into the thoughts of Einstein, Ludwig Lewisohn, William Blake, and Montaigne's *Essays.*

The "Zarathustrian principle of life is opposed by the principle of love," for example. There are short stories such as *God's Daughters*, and meditative essays such as "A Portrait of Burroughs as a Critic." A novella utilized the turbulent experiences of his experiences, both good and bad. He drew on Lucien Carr's manslaughter charge for killing David Kammerer in a 1945 collaboration with Burroughs, *I Wish I Were You: The Philip Tourian Story* (which staggered on for fifty-three pages, and was later corrected by Kerouac before its abandonment). Another was *Orpheus Emerged,* which depicted people from his life under pseudonyms. However, none of these well-intended efforts satisfied him. Ultimately their only purpose was to bolster what had become an impressive word count for a man of twenty-two.

It was only one summer before meeting Neal Cassady that Kerouac recognized that the "artist of today" must reject human toil for artistic toil in realizing that art was a mainstay of personality. He must be more emphatically a being than a human—part prophet and part martyr with a touch of the "human devil." The true artist is obligated to face all crimes, evils, and perversions as the penalty for his calling. Echoing Picasso, Kerouac realized an artist wore the "face of the future" while enduring solitude. Lastly, the true artist cannot expect gratuitous elevation over other men. By realizing this, he was preparing for the rigors of the remainder of his life. Life on the road would bring him obscurity, poverty, and utter disappointment, if little else.

In the months preceding his first departure for the west, Kerouac looked for a job on a shipping vessel that would take him far from America. Though it was also in response to the demands of his family that he contribute to the family's income, it would also break him free from his work which threatened to stagnate despite his efforts.

AMERICAN SOJOURNER

On June 26, 1947, Kerouac departed Ozone Park for his first cross-country trip, to be made famous in the first part of *On the Road.* The road would take its toll and exude mystery; Kerouac would learn the savage demands of hunger, thirst, and desire. "Everything belongs to me because I am poor." He would not be discouraged, at least for the majority of the remainder of his life, for he had made his decision, the kind proclaimed by Yeats in "The Choice":

> The intellect of man is forced to choose
> Perfection of the life, or of the work,
> And if it take the second must refuse
> A heavenly mansion, raging in the dark.

For Kerouac, "perfection of the work" would dominate an imperfect life. The other conflict he faced is whether his art was worth the difficulties his life would face. Agreeing wholeheartedly with Spengler's belief in *The Decline of the*

West that the Western world was under the spell of a tremendous "optical illusion," Kerouac was attracted to such passages as:

> Everyone *demands* something of the rest. We say "thou shalt" in the conviction that so-and-so in fact will, can and must be changed or fashioned or arranged comfortably to the order, and our belief both in the efficacy of, and in our title to give, such orders is unshakable. *That,* and nothing short of it, *is*, *for* us, morale. In the ethics of the West everything is direction, claim to power, will to affect the distant. (Spengler, *The Decline of the West I,* 341)

Society's quest to validate itself alienated Kerouac to the quick, and his choice to partake only of what would further his artistic destiny colored the best and worst of his days. The rest of his life fell by the wayside—politics, family, economic preservation, and the expectations of assuming a comprehensible identity. This marked him as an eccentric dissident from not only the stifling prison of 1950s conformity, but also from those individuals unwilling to forgo their own comfort and their nine-to-five jobs. He wrote in the fall of 1947:

> It is well understood that a human being, rather than he should give himself over to a life of struggling for

> himself alone, "earning his living" grimly, "owing no debts," doing nothing else in his life, should perhaps better and more beautifully disport himself in this world by creating, inventing, dedicating, producing and presenting the world he lives in with the fruits of some personal contribution. All the world admires a Henry Ford, an Edison—they were more than rich and successful, they gave something back with interest. A John Barrymore, with interest, gives back his talent; a Shakespeare, a Dostoevsky, a Mark Twain, a Beethoven—all kinds of men, similar in one great respect, that they transcend their own lives and give something back. Compare this kind of man with the grubbing little shopkeeper—grudging, grumbling, a thousand grubby adjectives to describe him! Compare this kind of man, this Marconi, this Copernicus, this Jesus Christ, who gazes beyond the horizon of his own day-by-day interests and contemplates a dream of contribution, to the shopkeeper snarling at the "wolf at his door." A lot of great men never had doors, and roamed with the very wolves themselves—and they managed, they lived, they ate, slept, loved, worked, they managed! (Windblown World, 118)

Considering America his "subject as a writer," it was Kerouac's priority to know "everything about it." He carefully prepared for his road trip with a volley of voluminous reading. At a small library in Manhattan, he sat at a table and browsed several books at once, taking notes from each and recording his gleanings in a notebook. In Francis Parkman's *The Oregon Trail: Sketches of Prairie and Rocky Mountain Life,* he admired the pencil sketches of Frederick Remington and the vivid descriptions of the prairies at dawn, the belt of the plains stretching under the vast starry sky, the Central Platte with its ever-present Pawnee threatening to "rob" the emigrants progressing deeper into the west. Surly hunters and trappers staked their claims on traveling hordes of buffalo, whose population was gradually thinning as the meadows they trampled dissipated into dust. The barren plains were littered with skinned, rotting hulks of slain beasts.

Kerouac read American history, the Revolutionary War specifically, and a biography of George Washington. Intent on becoming knowledgeable about "every state in the USA," he read page after page, noting geographical landmarks like lakes, bays, mountains and cities. However, he realized, no amount of "conquer[ing] knowledge" from a book could take the place of the actual experience.

In letter to William S. Burroughs, now hunkered down fifty-five miles north of Houston in New Waverly, Texas, Kerouac privied him to his plans. In that remote location, whose primary residents existed on lumbering, Burroughs, assisted by Herbert Huncke, planned to grow and profit from the marijuana plants and opium poppies he planted. In the letter, Kerouac indicated his desire for his old friend to communicate to Neal Cassady and Allen Ginsberg that he intended on arriving in Denver by the twenty-third of July. Covering ground for his intentions in the Midwest, he now made his plans for the west coast.

Henri Cru had moved to San Francisco and, during a brief stop in New York with a good stash of Panama Red, he had invited Kerouac there to look for work on the ships that regularly sailed from the port. He had recently returned from sea and now he was even more adamant about getting Jack to ship out with him. Also, they wrote. The five-page screenplay that they collaborated on, titled *Blood and Paper or Lunchtime Wake,* derived from an original story contributed by Cru. It never came to fruition and remains to this day unpublished.

Kerouac had toyed with the idea of moving to the west eventually, but never seriously. His reasons for escaping the city were multifold; he felt stale there, unaccomplished, and he was tired of the negativity and overall pessimism of the circles he traveled in. Other friends and acquaintances of Kerouac's had also departed in the spring of 1947. Hal Chase had concluded his studies at Columbia and returned home to Denver. Ed White, though he hadn't graduated, chose to spend the summer in Denver as well. Lucien Carr, now at United Press International, had neither the inclination nor the time to carouse with his former Columbia associates.

Allen Ginsberg was also planning to move away, at least temporarily, to be closer to Neal Cassady, whom he was still in love with. Ginsberg's letters to Cassady came fast, constant, and furious. Cassady destroyed the letters lest his relations with Ginsberg be exposed to Carolyn, LuAnne, or anybody else. The contents of Ginsberg's letters tended to be graphic, illustrating the extent of his lust for Cassady and how he would act on it. Cassady, however, only expressed concern about the overcoats he wanted Ginsberg to send to him, some books, and Ginsberg's poetry he could claim as his own.

After Cassady's departure, Ginsberg attempted to find a psychoanalyst. He wrote a letter to an Austrian-American psychiatrist named Wilhelm Reich, who believed that there was a form of physical energy that permeated the atmosphere and in living matter. His teachings brought him to the attention of the Food and Drug Administration, which issued an injunction against the "orgone accumulators" he was selling (Burroughs owned one). To Reich, Ginsberg wrote: "I have had long periods of depression, guilt feelings—disguised mostly as a sort of Kafkian sordidness of sense of self, melancholy and the whole gamut I suppose." An assistant of Reich's wrote back to Ginsberg, referring him to a number of different Reichian physicians in Manhattan. Ginsberg sought the help of one, Dr. A. Allan Cott. However, Ginsberg quit after he was advised to lay off the marijuana.

Ginsberg finished off the spring term and made plans to go to Texas and visit Burroughs. After that visit, he planned to see Cassady to reinvigorate their passion, though Cassady had warned him in June about meeting a "wonderful girl."

Though Cassady did not respond similarly, he teased Ginsberg enough to give him the illusion that, despite Cassady's marriage to LuAnne, Ginsberg could win Cassady over with his promise to make him a writer and to educate him with poetry.

Cassady had written Kerouac in April, to tell him that he hadn't had time to be "concerned with America and all it means at the moment" (he was also preparing for a trip to Las Vegas for gambling). He urged the perpetually paranoid Kerouac not to "take on a defensive, apologetic air which we both feel only because of a self-imposed sense of obligation." His solution was simple: "Let's forget all this shit and just scribble to each other what [we] feel, not what we think." In the interim, Cassady had found a job laboring ten hours a day digging ditches and mixing cement. He planned to leave for Trinidad, Colorado, at the end of May and to stay until June 15, and from there visit Burroughs in Texas.

ONE GREAT RED LINE

On the seventeenth of July, Kerouac closed the door behind him at his Ozone Park apartment, gathered his bearings, and began his first serious trek across the continent. It was a significant period for the country. In July 1947, the United States government formed the Central Intelligence Agency. The Marshall Plan had gone into effect the previous month to assist European countries in rising from the ashes of destruction wrought from the war. On the evening of July 3, 1947, Dan Wilmot was sitting on the front porch of his home in Roswell, New Mexico, with his wife when they spotted a bright light in the evening sky. In their estimate, the 25-foot object was flying from the southeast and had to be traveling at least five hundred miles an hour before vanishing to the northwest. Cover-ups, government involvement, and stifled inquests gave rise to conspiracy theories that exist to this day.

Just twenty-three miles from Kerouac, a developer began transforming 1,200 acres of potato fields in Island Trees, New York, and called it Levittown. The homes spread over this tract of land consisted initially of Cape Cod–style homes priced at a little over $10,000 with a mortgage averaging $67 a month, just right for the postwar veterans who lined up in droves to fulfill their American dream. Levitt's solution to speed productivity and reduce labor costs was simple; he offered only two basic house types. The tenants had the choice to rent their home initially before opting to purchase it.

By 1950, *Time* magazine estimated, Levitt and Sons were responsible for manufacturing one out of every eight houses in the country. The advances the United States was making at the time did not go unnoticed by other nations. The postwar boom in housing, the availability of education for the veterans, and the shift in art and science branded the country as the "First New Nation." It was the only country that began anew in the spirit of innovation and invention. The promise of peace and prosperity garnished the returning soldiers' lives. Levittown, in all of its bleak sameness, was, for now, the American Dream.

Kerouac, a veteran, did not harbor the same sentiments (though his medical discharge was for psychiatric reasons, it was still "Honorable"). Though he coddled the notion of having a wife and children and would later detail his wish to Cassady of buying a ranch in Colorado, he had his priorities. His "American Dream" lie in a fast car and a finished novel.

Kerouac was dead set against borrowing any more money from his mother. Hitchhiking would cut some of the expenses of travel and he would wing the rest when the time came. Frugality and good planning were the rules of his journey, which would set a precedent for the rest of his travels during his lifetime. Planning on arriving in Denver in one week, he began by taking the Seventh Avenue subway all the way to 242nd Street, where he boarded a trolley that took him to Yonkers. Holding out his thumb, he successfully solicited a series of rides north along the banks of the Hudson River. However, he soon ended up under a bridge as the rain poured into the dark vast hollow of Bear Mountain.

Kerouac had arrived, as he planned, at Route 6, fifty miles north of New York City, where it snakes out suddenly from the expanse of rural Connecticut. On Bear Mountain, the first section of the Appalachian Trail, the tumult of black clouds and rolling thunder was at once daunting and exciting, but it put Kerouac seriously behind schedule. The road was empty. In duress he accepted a ride from the first set of lights that swept out of the darkness. They were going north, taking him ten miles in the wrong direction, to Newburgh, New York. In a Newburgh bus depot he bought a ticket that bounced him back to Penn Station. It was discouraging, yet he was eager to move on. Peeling bills from his precious bankroll of fifty dollars, he bought a bus ticket to Chicago.

The ride, described in *On the Road* as "ordinary" right down to its crying babies and cooing mothers, rolled westward. Unlike Cassady's exciting bus adventure from New York City to Denver in March 1946, the considerably more reserved and modest Kerouac didn't score any sexual conquests with young female travelers. His uneventful journey dropped him off at the bustling Loop in Chicago. Exhausted, he found an inexpensive YMCA room and killed some time listening to the fervent bebop that was by now taking the country by storm.

Bebop, condensed to *bop,* was a radical take on jazz exposition, the birth of modern jazz. Melody was secondary to improvisations based on harmony and chordal arrangements. The music was complex and, at first, hard to take aurally. Kerouac recounts the advent of bop: "[T]hen it happened—bop happened—the bird flew in—minds went in—on the streets thousands of new-type hepcats in red shirts and some goatees and strange-looking cowboys from the West with boots and belts, and the girls began to disappear from the street . . ." ("The Beginning of Bop"). Whereas big band had swing, bebop was all about speed and virtuosity. Bebop bands had performers as opposed to players and each performer was expected to indulge in extended soloing and individual expression (akin to the new dance form at the beginning of the decade called the jitterbug that also allowed individual expression).

Its appeal to the audience of the time was limited. Many people who were accustomed to big band music like Ellington and Louis Armstrong avoided it. Bop had a number of stigmas attached to it; the whiff of pot and the dreadful aura of morphine and heroin addiction attached itself like barnacles to the nascent art form that fearlessly crested the wave of American culture. Kerouac, an avid supporter of the genre since its inception, later incorporated the stylistic elements of its spontaneity and free form into his writing.

One of the most potent leaders of this movement was becoming a favorite of Kerouac's. Charlie Parker had been experimenting with bebop since 1939. During a performance of "Cherokee," he had figured out a way to play what was inside of his head by scaffolding chords based on the song's harmonies. By 1947 he was at the peak of his powers. With drummer Max Roach and trumpeter Miles Davis, he had a band that was able to keep up with his rapid, driven improvisations. Parker's skill of improvisation served as a potent influence on Kerouac's later works.

A truck driver in Joliet brought Kerouac to the state line of Illinois; from there his progress is detailed in *On the Road.* An older lady who needed her car driven to Davenport, Iowa, took him on a trip that was memorable for his first glimpse of the wide banks of the Mississippi River on the eastern border of Iowa. Davenport, one of the only cities on the Mississippi that chooses not to use a permanent floodwall or levee was the birthplace of one of his favorite jazz musicians, Bix Beiderbecke. Most notable was Kerouac's claim to his mother, immortalized in *On the Road*: "I went to sit in the bus station and think this over. I ate another apple pie and ice cream; that's practically all I ate all the way across the country. I knew it was nutritious and it was delicious, of course." A penny postcard bought at a "rickety Indian store" and sent on July 24 to his mother said that he planned on being in Colorado that evening. Later, from Cheyenne, Wyoming, amid "Wild West Week," he sent her another postcard sharing his impressive progress, six hundred miles in one day: "am now 2/3 of the way to California, money holding out. Having great trip."

He was west at last.

DEAN AND CAMILLE

As Kerouac trekked through the Midwestern plains, Neal Cassady was juggling the arduous affections of two women and one man: he remained sexually active with LuAnne, his now-estranged wife; he courted Carolyn Robinson, a former Bennington coed, with strained gentility; and he tried defusing Ginsberg's obsessive sexual desires while befriending him. At times he caved into Ginsberg, if only to just get himself off.

Cassady had met Carolyn (Camille in *On the Road*) on the day of his arrival from New York City in March, introduced by Bill Tomson (Roy Johnson in *On the Road*). Carolyn was an artist in a master's program at the University of Denver. Tomson, to Carolyn, was a "nuisance." He sought her out every day on campus despite her disdain for his shallow conversation, which included boasting about Cassady's antics. Like Hal Chase, Tomson was consumed by Cassady's boundless energy, swaggering confidence, and unswerving work ethic. He was well aware of Carolyn's serious academic side, and so, to gain her approval, he assured her that Cassady was a student at Columbia University, where he had spent time in the good company of an Ivy League athlete and a gifted poet.

According to LuAnne, Cassady's arrival brought him back to her arms and into her hotel room. After a few nights in the room, LuAnne's stepfather intervened, attempting to take her away from Cassady, thus gaining custody of their underaged daughter. However, a Denver judge ruled that parental authority was nullified once the child was married (even if she *was* jailbait married to an ex-con). This bolstered LuAnne's independence. Cassady went out and got a job, as did she.

According to Carolyn, however, Tomson appeared at her

door with the T-shirted Cassady the same day his Denver bus arrived from the east. Tomson had lured Cassady with the promise that comely Carolyn had an impressive collection of Lester Young records. Though this was not the case, she did have others, which Cassady flipped through shortly after arriving there, encouraging her with his admiration of them. There was Nat King Cole, Harry James, the Dorsey Brothers, Stan Kenton, Artie Shaw; one album in particular caught Cassady's eye and he inquired about it.

It was by Josh White, the American singer known for his gospel and blues renditions in the folk circuit. White's involvement in the civil rights movement during the 1940s resulted in his blacklisting by the House Committee on Un-American Activities, only lifted after he testified of possible communist strains infiltrated through the entertainment industry. Her possession of them was a radical gesture on her part, as she thought at the time, and she sensed Cassady's "empathy" toward her when she explained who the singer was and how she knew of him a "little." When Cassady asked if Tomson and Carolyn had plans, she protested having been burdened of late by theatrical design projects. Her desire "to see more of this man" one-upped her work ethic, however, and obeying the advice of her spirit she got her coat.

Cassady packed his clothes and impulsively handed Carolyn a love poem, saying that he had written it. She could see already that he wasn't capable of such verse and later figured out it was Allen Ginsberg's. Walking to a bus station, they took a bus that dropped them off at a hotel more suited for the penurious likes of Cassady's hobo father than upscale Carolyn. Inside the room, Cassady dropped his suitcase on the unmade bed littered with female articles of clothing. Later at a café, he argued with a girl who worked there. When Carolyn found out that the girl was Cassady's wife, LuAnne, she was stunned that both Tomson and he had strung her along without the slightest hint that he was married. Unruffled by the fact that Carolyn was on to him, Cassady led her to a record-playing booth, in which she noticed his enthusiasm for jazz. He alerted her to the occasional riff and the driven backbeat. Turned off yet intrigued, she remained with him for the time being.

When LuAnne arrived from her shift, Cassady left Carolyn for a few minutes for a quickie in LuAnne's hotel room, sullying his genteel demeanor. When Bill Tomson signaled to Carolyn that it was time to go, she was relieved. As she was leaving, Cassady held up his hand and stuck up two fingers. He turned again and faced the others who had joined them during the evening. She had no idea what that meant, but she was relieved to be finally home and rid of Tomson. She washed her face and put on pajamas, ready for bed. Lowering the bed from its hideaway, she was about to climb in when there was a barely perceptible knock on the door. The clock read 2:00 AM. Two fingers. Neal Cassady. She opened the door and there he stood holding his suitcase: "He eased past my catatonic figure, dropped his suitcase and calmly seated himself on the couch, his knees brushing the foot of the bed. I grabbed my robe, squirmed into it and sat on the opposite end of the couch, ardently wishing I had not lowered that bed."

The advent of Carolyn marked the loss, however diffident it was in the first place, of Cassady's interest in Ginsberg as a lover. Cassady admired her for the same reasons he was attracted to Ginsberg, a "sort of awareness or intuitive sense of understanding which is our (yours and mine) chief forte" (Cassady to Ginsberg, June 1947). Preparing Ginsberg for their imminent meeting, he portrayed Carolyn as having a "lack of cynicism, artificial sophistication and sterility in her creative make-up." Though he wasn't a fan of her strait-lacedness, he saw it as a challenge, one from which he would periodically test her. Carolyn recalls: "Neal saw I didn't suit his temperament. The challenge was to perform with me in accordance with my squareness. As the challenge with Ginsberg was to cope with his queerness." Cassady urged Ginsberg not to be "dependent" on him, and that he would be the same toward Ginsberg. By the time of Kerouac's arrival, the Cassady circus was in full swing: LuAnne (who he urged not to hurry back from Los Angeles by letter), Carolyn, a pair of sisters (named Gullion), and the emotionally and physically needy Ginsberg. Carolyn was not aware of the depth of their former relations.

DENVER

On July 28 Kerouac arrived in Denver for a "rest," a temporary stopover before continuing his trip to San Francisco. He was already broke and he determined that he would need another $25 in order to take a bus to California. Hitchhiking over the mountains and across the desert was out of the question. For now he planned no more than ten days in Denver, until the money reached him via Western Union and then moving on.

His first impression was one of wonder. The geology of the west contrasted remarkably with the hilly east. It was nothing he had read about in the books he studied in Manhattan. Peaks of mountains skirted the western horizon; the air thinner exuding a greater degree of purity than he was used to in smoggy Manhattan.

On arrival, Kerouac sought out Hal Chase with the help of Chase's mother. Chase picked him up in his Ford coupe. Though Kerouac was eager to find Cassady, he discovered that Chase had become disenchanted with Neal, something Cassady had sensed in an earlier letter to Ginsberg. Cassady was also aware of his own need for emotional distance, and that he could effortlessly detach himself from any kind of emotional entanglement. This destructive current allowed him to pursue anything he wanted.

Chase knew nothing of Cassady's whereabouts nor of Ginsberg's presence. The fact is, Kerouac's stay in Denver was largely uneventful save for his introduction to Carolyn

Robinson, his observations of Denver life for use in later fiction, and a few days spent in the company of Ed White, Hal Chase, and Allan Temko (another Columbia friend, "Roland Major" in *On the Road*). The split between the group around Cassady and the one around Chase suited the polarity of Kerouac's temperament. His abilities as a writer and a scholar made him suitable company for either. Temko and White, and the brother and sister Bob and Beverly Burford (Babe and Ray Rawlins in *On the Road*) suggested Jack read from his journal, which ignited their creative sensibilities and perhaps inspired them to attend to their separate projects anew. Beverly was immediately attracted to Kerouac; his beefy physique, startling blue eyes, jet-black hair, and handsomeness were frosting on the cake of his mind.

Ginsberg's withdrawal signaled the end of the old order, the New Vision, the friendship in New York City that had occasioned so many late night discussions of writing and literature. Consumed with his desperate need for expression (both poetic and sexual) and his desire for a relationship, Ginsberg was not entirely suited for Kerouac's desire to shed himself of such ambiguity. Ginsberg documented his anguish over Neal in his journal, detailing his dreams to free himself "from the coldness of this present moment" (Ginsberg journal, 192). Late nights into early morning he lay awake waiting for Neal to come to him, and when he didn't, Ginsberg turned to his journal: "Neal has not come to me, and I think that if at this moment he came, if I were not to throw him out of doors, I would let myself play love with him, out of sheer boredom, having nothing else to do" (ibid, 192). Ginsberg had a job at the May Co. department store, and a basement apartment on Grant Street. As Ginsberg retreated inward, Kerouac sought external experience, having already retreated as far into introversion as he was willing to go during *The Town and the City's* composition.

Kerouac and Ginsberg discovered that their mutual friends were all very friendly and intelligent, boasting a sophisticated demeanor and a humility that they had assumed was only available in New York City. There were also drugs and plenty of them. Kerouac found that Benzedrine was readily available. In the black section of town, he and Ed White listened to music in the jazz joints. On Larimer Street, the old haunt of Cassady and his father, poolhalls, beer joints, and inexpensive food, was available. Yet, on any direction out of the city, the hot, unforgiving landscape became wild, monotonous and, to the uninitiated, dangerous.

Ginsberg alerted Kerouac to the three-way relationship Cassady was handling with seemingly dexterous ease. Carolyn Robinson was in one hotel, LuAnne was in another, Ginsberg was miserably holed up in his apartment. Somehow, Neal still held a steady job.

LuAnne had still harbored hope that Neal would relinquish his extracurricular lifestyle and come back to her. She recalls: "Neal and I had a very dramatic scene on the grass at the Capital Building. Neal was telling me goodbye, and I was crying and telling him that I couldn't live without him. It was just a young girl pouring her heart out. I really and truly thought I would die. At that point I had no visions of any life at all with Neal gone."

It was typical teenage angst, abruptly severed by a dose of Neal Cassady's reality fix: "I don't ever want to see you begging or crying like that for a man again." He told her that just because he was going to Texas with Ginsberg, it didn't mean he felt anything less for her. LuAnne and Neal went to the pad Cassady kept in the rooming house. At four o'clock in the morning, Ginsberg appeared. They all went to bed together until Carolyn Robinson showed up, prompted by Bill Tomson to catch Cassady in the act. Says LuAnne Henderson, "She walked in and caught me in bed with Neal, and she just went insane." Cassady jumped up and tried to explain being caught with his wife (!) and to placate the three of them, each possessing a mutual interest in Neal Cassady as lover, husband, and friend. At some point, Cassady assured Carolyn that he was in the process of divorcing LuAnne.

With such drama in his life, Kerouac was probably a relief of reason for Cassady, who was genuinely pleased to be with him once again. Absent the needy trio of Carolyn, LuAnne, and Ginsberg, Cassady could show another side of himself that didn't require so much *giving.*

Kerouac's introduction to Carolyn came one day when Ginsberg accompanied him to Cassady's room at the Hotel

Colburn. Ginsberg knocked on Cassady's door, but suddenly ducked out of sight into an alley when he realized Carolyn was there. (Carolyn had nothing against Ginsberg, and at times even tolerated his company with Cassady, though it was an uneasy companionship.) Cassady opened the door, covering himself with a towel while Carolyn lay behind him in a state of undress, a picture postcard of Cassady's mythology, introduced Carolyn to Kerouac, and then, after dressing and assuring her that he'd be back, left with him. As if making a concerted effort to complicate his life even further, Cassady's goal was the Gullion sisters, Rita and Helen, both nurses, who invited Bob Burford over as well and ultimately a party ensued. When things got cooking, Neal ducked out for an hour to keep his promise to Carolyn.

Kerouac was intrigued by Carolyn almost instantly. When she rehearsed for her two plays at a theater company, he attended each rehearsal and was complimentary without being patronizing toward her performance. She noted Kerouac's constant scribbling in his notebook no matter what the occasion. When they were with Cassady, she asked Kerouac to dance with her. Kerouac whispered tensely, "It's too bad . . . Neal saw you first." Kerouac was single, handsome, and perhaps willing to open his soul to her but beneath his best intentions his artist's heart would ultimately move on.

By the end of July, Kerouac had grown restless and was eager to resume his journey. He wrote his mother, "Now I want to get on to San Francisco and make some money, I haven't a cent left and I'll need $25 [author's note: $25 more than what he said he asks from his "aunt" in *On the Road*] to take a bus to California from here, because hitch-hiking is impossible across the desert and the mountains." He directed her to the Western Union office in Brooklyn to wire the money to 1475 Cherry Street in Denver, the address of Ed White's father. Kerouac described his time in Denver to his mother as one of buoyant joy and unhinged energy: enjoying the company of his "ten girlfriends," indulging in steaming slabs of venison steak, or tagging along for a drive thirty-five miles west from Denver to the gold-mining-era town of Central City. He was brimming over with an optimism that he had never felt in Manhattan.

Kerouac went to Central City with Beverly and Bob Burford (in her employer's car), the Temkos, and Ed White. Perhaps knowing Kerouac's love for Beethoven, they decided to take him to a performance of *Fidelio* during the Central City Opera House's Summer Festival Season. The recently refurbished opera house, the nation's fifth oldest, had been reopened fifteen years before his attendance there. It sat among a cluster of Victorian homes. Kerouac, attired in a suit, was absorbed by the melodrama and sweeping score. Afterward they went out for an evening of carousing.

Kerouac was disappointed that he had narrowly missed seeing Cassady and Ginsberg in Central City the night before. Though the others, especially Bob Burford and Allan

Temko, failed to see Cassady's attraction for Kerouac, they accepted his quirky taste as the price one had to pay to keep such unique company. They came from families with money, and Neal had been raised by a Larimer Street wino. Kerouac was able to distill from each what he ultimately needed for his fiction. He couldn't see what wasn't charming about the down-and-outers, but he also didn't see anything special about those who had money.

Cassady was no saint, he knew, but to Kerouac, saints weren't necessarily pure and free of temptation and sin. This, according to Kerouac, was a sainthood perfectly in line with Dostoevsky's, a man he thought of as a saint. "Everybody seems to assume that saints are perfect. It seems to me that saints are the most imperfect, tortured, doubtful human beings in this world. They are not perfect at all. They sin as much as anybody else, at first, and then later you don't see their sins. You can't live without sinning. The thing about a saint is that he understands crime and sinning better than anyone else, from experience and long meditation. The only thing perfect about a saint is his doubt. Saintliness is perfection of doubt" (Journal, August 11, 1947). Twice in *Visions of Cody,* Kerouac calls Cassady a "brother." "Cody is the brother I lost—he could very well have been my brother instead of the actual one I had who died—did he die a dead death?—or a living death—?" (VOC, 318). He becomes, to Kerouac, the "arbiter of what I think" (VOC, 320).

In his last days in Denver, Kerouac spent more time on Larimer Street. He had the idea of searching for Cassady's lost father, "the father we never found," an idea that would recur in all future incarnations of *On the Road.* He spent these last hours with Ginsberg and Cassady, who introduced him to Al Hinkle, along with an array of other Larimer Street regulars.

When Kerouac received his wired money, he bought his bus ticket. Knowing full well that hitchhiking through the Rockies, the Hot Basin, and the Sierra Nevadas was madness, he opted to see the rest of the American West through a bus window. Although Kerouac called Cassady from a pay phone, it was Ed White who saw him off at the station. Cassady's vague promise of joining him in California would not come to be. Kerouac realized that, with all of craziness with Carolyn, he hadn't maintained a solid conversation with Cassady for more than a few minutes.

The bus crept through towns, cities, and desert. By dawn, it had reached the Crossroads of the West and the birthplace of Neal Cassady Jr., Salt Lake City, which had been founded by pioneering Mormons in 1847. By dusk, the bus had reached Reno, Nevada, and the Sierras, beautiful beyond words. Kerouac missed having Cassady around to bring life to the moment. His presence had a way of making any setting come alive with possibilities.

The next day Kerouac felt the "warm, palmy air" and he instantly knew that he was in California. First it was the mountain town of Truckee, notable for the doomed Donner

Party. By dawn it was the "sleepy lights of Frisco." When the bus pulled into Market and Fourth Street, Kerouac was fast asleep.

'FRISCO

Kerouac knew he was at least two weeks late in meeting Henri Cru. Gaunt, hungry, and eager to stretch his legs after riding in a bus for several days, Kerouac wandered the streets of San Francisco. He was badgered by vagrants asking for dimes. He crossed the Golden Gate Bridge into Marin County, one of the first counties settled in California. Marin is now one of the leading high-technology areas in California, the home of George Lucas's Skywalker Ranch and also the sprawling 432-acre San Quentin Prison, the oldest prison in California (opened in July 1852). With skiing, mountain biking, and climbing, swimming in the Pacific Ocean, San Francisco to the south and Sonoma County at its northern border, there was plenty to distract Kerouac whenever he grew bored of Cru and his girlfriend's constant bickering.

Meanwhile, Cassady and Ginsberg had hitchhiked to New Waverly, Texas, reaching there on August 30, 1947. Huncke tried to cobble together a bed for Ginsberg and Cassady by binding together two army cots, without success. Cassady refused to help Huncke, whose skin was scarred with boils and hives. Burroughs, for his part, couldn't care less *where* Ginsberg and Cassady slept. Peeved at his host for not being more proactive about their living quarters, Ginsberg tried to help Huncke. It was a miserable effort and served to bookend a period of absolute misery for the lovelorn Ginsberg. Kerouac incorporated Cassady's account of this in *Visions of Cody:*

> Irwin [pseudonym for Allen Ginsberg] his only concern was building this bed for where we was gonna sleep that night. . .and there was two cots, see, and that was what we were going to sleep on, but Huck [pseudonym for Huncke] and Irwin had the big idea to join the two cots, and that entitled a great deal of work, you see they were Army cots securely stapled together, and had to break all that, and pull all the front whole side of both of the cots, and then put them together." (*Visions of Cody,* 140)

Ginsberg, simultaneously depressed and angry, enlisted on a merchant marine vessel. Risking being late for the new semester at Columbia, Ginsberg boarded a vessel and was gone, twenty days crossing the Atlantic, to Dakar, Africa. On their last night together, Cassady, stoned out of his mind on barbiturates, found a girl recently discharged from a mental hospital. She helped him climb the stairs to the hotel room he had rented for his last night with the poet. After Ginsberg left, Cassady shot letters north to

Carolyn in a desperate plea to have her back. His other letters were sent to Jack.

Kerouac found out, shortly after meeting up with Cru, that the merchant marine job would never come to pass, either because his luck had run out or because he had been duped by Henri Cru, who wanted Kerouac to help him write a screenplay. Whatever the case, he was consumed, as usual, with his work-in-progress languishing unattended on his desk back at Ozone Park. He envisioned New York bathed in the golden light of October. Kerouac's attraction to the month of October, especially evident in his juvenilia and in the working draft of *The Town and the City,* stems from his love for New England autumns. In October, Lowell and its surroundings are aglow with the reds, yellows, oranges, purples of deciduous trees. Billowing smoke imbues the air as it lazily drifts from chimney stacks. The snapping chill of winter is tasted as it saps the last remnants of summer from earth and sky.

October is also of importance to French Canadians; during that month, French Canadian Catholics dedicate their days to the rosary, fumbling their shiny beads through restless fingers, uttering "The Lord's Prayer," "Hail Holy Queen," "the Apostles Creed," "the Sorrowful Mysteries," the "Glorious Mysteries," the "Luminous Mysteries," and the "Joyful Mysteries" into "decades," completing the rosary cycle. Each "mystery" had its place in the burgeoning pages of Kerouac's notebook. Interspersed are prayers, which often evoke the mysteries of life, both joyful and sad, and of death. In his knapsack were rosary beads given to him by his mother. Though it is unknown whether Kerouac actually said a formal rosary cycle, he wrote of them throughout his life. His appreciation of the Catholic rosary indicated noble constants in his religious mysticism.

On August 10, the day of his arrival, he quoted Melville's *Moby Dick* in his journal: "There now your insular isle of the Manhattoes, belted round by wharves, bound round by flashing tides." His *The Town and the City* character, Peter Martin, was "street-drowned and Brooklyn-slain," and "sorrow" imbued his "soul." Kerouac extended the idea, picturing his character on the road, perhaps in the middle of Nebraska, standing in the hot sun, as cars flew by him from Texas, California, Ohio, and Georgia, perhaps saying to one another, "Look! A hitchhiker!" On the day of his arrival in San Francisco, Kerouac happened upon the perfect ending to *The Town and the City.* Peter Martin's life in the novel, up to now, perfectly mirrored Kerouac's. The death of the Martin family patriarch, George, frees Peter to take to the road, as Leo Kerouac's death in 1946 had freed Jack to take his role as a writer seriously, as well as his responsibility of taking care of his mother (even though Gabrielle was oftentimes supporting *him*).

The other idea that came to Kerouac was of the insertion of Greek myth. He draws from *Apollodorus's Library,* which details the relations between Uranus (Great Father Sky) and

Gaia (Great Mother Earth). In Sir J. G. Frazer's translation of *Apollodorus's Library*, Apollodorus describes this pantheon as such:

> Sky (Uranos) was the first who ruled over the whole world. And having wedded Earth (Gaia), he begat first the Hundred-handed . . . After these, Earth bore him the Cyclopses . . . But them Sky bound and cast into Tartarus . . . And he begat children by Earth, to wit, the Titans . . . and youngest of all, Cronus . . . But Earth, grieved at the destruction of her children, who had been cast into Tartarus . . .

These entries in his journal were later transformed into the closing chapters of *The Town and the City* to emphasize a dramatic setting: "gold-furious and golden beautiful in October this was the setting for the drama of human things and of human sorrow."

Kerouac later infused a synthesis of Spengler's *fellaheen* people with a sense of the originating forces that thrived in the lands he traveled. Whether it was Lowell, California, Greenland, or Mexico, Kerouac united all in his own peculiar monomyth. The idea that the Earth is an "Indian thing" makes its first appearance during Kerouac's short California stay. Acutely aware that his boyhood in Pawtucketville put him close to the sacred grounds of the Pawtucket Indians, he used this idea in his mature work: the impressive backdrop of the Pawtucket Falls, the tenement-riddled Pawtucketville bordering the shore of the Merrimack River where it elbows north from the south (eloquently captured in the opening pages of *The Town and the City*). Kerouac began envisioning the whole of America, and not just his hometown of Lowell, in mythical proportions. All that he seemingly lacked, with the weak exception of Peter Martin who stood in for that need, was a mythical prototype. His friendship with Neal Cassady fulfilled that. Throughout the next two years, he would employ an arsenal of stock characters for his new *road* novel. Kerouac's need for an ancient civilization to fully realize his vision of the *fellaheen* would be fulfilled later in his travels into the heart of Mexico.

Kerouac began appreciating an understanding of Indian culture, an interest that persisted through all of the subsequent drafts of *On the Road*. Prayer sticks, prayer wheels, and the thought that the Indians were the "source of mankind" and "fathers of it" bolstered Kerouac's naive image of them as helpless beneath the rolling wheels of civilization's progress.

During his early days in California, Kerouac entertained the idea of writing a screenplay tentatively titled "Christmas in New York." Both Henri Cru's sister and his father had contacts in Hollywood, and his plan was to get his writer friend to do the bulk of the work and then, together, they could rake in the proceeds. However, the screenplay was a pale imitation at best of a fully realized movie idea. Kerouac's forte was novel-writing: an epic novel with sweeping narration, flesh-and-blood characters imitative of Balzac, who he felt was the "most amazing writer that ever lived." Kerouac believed that Balzac was able to perfectly express his fertile imagination with the bleakness of reality. Also, Balzac was "all wrapped in huge creation," and "full of worldly knowledge," like Kerouac at times, and despite the warping specter of loneliness, he remained "passionate in his nightwork." Though Kerouac felt Dostoevsky was a greater writer, Balzac was always on "speaking terms with the ultimate issues of what we call mankind." Balzac's accumulated efforts were "amazing" because he never "allowed his soul to develop, in the interests of knowing more about the greedy nature of men, even as he knew it were better for himself." Balzac was formidable, for his chief preoccupation in his writing was the "squandering passions of men, nothing else." During Kerouac's moody broodings about writers and their art, he envisioned Balzac in his "grave, sleeping a *greedy sleep*."

During his second day in California, Kerouac pondered a lifelong dream of owning a horse and extended it to the idea of owning a ranch someday. The West held a sacred fascination to him, an inherent freedom in its open spaces, where he could realize his dream. He dreamed of a life of simplicity, a sapling idea sprung from the great tree of Henry David Thoreau's philosophy of simplicity and self-reliance. Emerson's self-reliance and Thoreau's credo of passive resistance were both manifested in Kerouac's sensibilities. He confided to his journal that nobody, neither friends nor family, knew of his great love for horses. His youthful dreams of being a jockey had vaporized when his stocky body exceeded the maximum height and weight allowed by the horse racing commission.

Owning a ranch, however, could partially realize his dream. Besides his writing, from which he never honestly thought to reap a living, he figured on riding horses to earn his wages. However, he was in need of a partner and, in the weeks to come, he began thinking of Neal Cassady. There would also have to be, in his mind, a woman of "simplicity" to share this life with. He wrote to Ed White, a month later, that he had inquired of Edie Parker, who was planning on living on a farm in Dexter, Michigan: "This is a mysterious enigmatic question that will dumb-found her for a week." This desperate search for a spouse of simplicity lasted until 1950 when Kerouac, on the verge of fully defining his mature writing style, married Joan Haverty (his second wife and mother to his only daughter, Janet Michelle Kerouac).

Kerouac would run afoul of his belief that his art came before all matters of domesticity and personal strife. Though he attracted, proposed, and in three cases married, the women would do more to complicate his life than arouse any sense of "simplicity."

THE FELLAHEEN EARTH

The *fellaheen,* people who work the soil with their bare hands, those who fashioned a living from the earth, with the ultimate prospect of returning to the soil whence they came, attracted the moral and mythical sensibilities of Kerouac. This idea began percolating conceptually for the "road" novel that began to fall into place over the next two years. The *fellah-people* were the opposite of the people tied to a Faustian ideal permeating Western culture, suggesting the likelihood of its death. What Kerouac extracted from *The Decline of the West* exerted great influence on all of his later writing: there is a futility to life that is locked into an ongoing cycle of "growth and decline and decay," a sentiment echoed in Buddhism, as he found later. His attraction to Spengler may be explained by Spengler's intuitive rather than scientific approach. This earned Spengler much ridicule from professional historians, just as Kerouac was later ridiculed for his radical writing style.

Kerouac also recognized something peculiar to and genuine in American literature as a whole (thus affecting the mood and rebellious tenor of *On the Road*). Its writers, whether Thoreau, Hawthorne, Melville, or Dickinson through the postmodernist efforts after World War II, were unique for their being "delved up from the veritable landscape and from the people in it, is indicative of any American soulfulness." Those that lacked such a connection suffered, in Kerouac's opinion. Henry James was a stellar example. James wrote of "discreet children" playing in the groomed gardens of stately mansions while their "elders unweave domestic dramas in the drawing room."

In contrast, in the rural theater of Twain, the rank and muddy banks of the Mississippi River were populated with unruly children and ruffians who were infinitely more vital to Kerouac than the "largest portraits of Beacon Street and Gramercy Square scions." The difference between the two, according to Kerouac, was that Twain's characterizations tended to "burn and glow and smolder darkly with mood, huge national *mood,* folk-wise and crude and simple." Kerouac likened Twain's creations to that of Homer, who delineated his characters starkly using stock epithets, elevating them to heroic proportions. Despite his disdain for the "leaver-outers" like Hemingway and F. Scott Fitzgerald, Kerouac still found that the pages of "Big Two-Hearted River," and portions of *The Great Gatsby* and *The Last Tycoon*, "trembled with unknown and unnamable mood-feelings." This happened to be one troublesome ravine Kerouac struggled to fill in his own work.

Kerouac felt the same about the junkies of New York on the fringe of existence: "they are gaunt and strange and melancholy, and they are bored." It wasn't their existence that interested him, it was the "mood" of their lives. This accounted for the "life of their lives" so successfully depicted by Dostoevsky, especially in the character of Raskolnikov in *Crime and Punishment*. Raskolnikov, huddled deep into the cloak of his guilt after committing a murder, expresses the humility of everyday existence; his eating, sleeping in a streetcar or walking "happily" down a street with "twinkling feet." Brooding upon this drove Kerouac into a creative frenzy and he became impatient to leave for New York at once to complete his novel: "It's the mere presence of life, not its drama, that drives me wondering and ecstatic to write about it—but how shall I write about it as no other man has written about it, unless I accept the initiative of complete and slightly "insane," originality, and do so in good earnest faith." Kerouac knew one thing for certain, that there were many ways to continue to write his novel, but there was only one way to write *The Town and the City,* and that was his way.

REMI BONCOEUR

Hank (Kerouac's nickname for Henri Cru) offered nothing for Kerouac but a poorly paid security job and a chance to ogle his comely girlfriend. Rowing a boat in the harbor, Kerouac relished the loneliness in the rusty confines of an anchored freighter (he even weighed the opportunity to sleep there for three days and three nights), where Cru's girl Dianne lounged nude in front of the men (much to the chagrin of the perpetually horny Kerouac). He wrote to Cassady: "We hired a rowboat and rowed out to an old ghost ship in the middle of the bay, an old freighter used as a buoy to warn navigators of the shallow water around there. We went aboard, Dianne took all her clothes off and sunned herself (she is one delectable little blonde, too, a natural blonde I am privileged to say), and Henry and I explored the ship with our flashlights, from captain's quarters to bilges" (Kerouac to Cassady, Sept. 13, 1947).

The elongated dormitories built especially for overseas construction workers required constant security. Sworn in by the Sausalito Police Department, Kerouac was made an "actual" officer of the law, who sometimes spent his days off going into San Francisco with his gun and badge. Once, his feelings of power exceeded his dignity and common sense: "Every time I meet a girl I whip out the old roscoe and pretend I'm a New York gangster and scare the hell out of them. Also, one night I pulled it out on a fag and told him I was 'Nanny-Beater Kelly' from Chicago." Kerouac makes no other mention of it in his journal, where he usually detailed everything he did. However, the adventure popped up in the scroll version of *On the Road.*

Outfitted with a uniform, whistle, and a .32 automatic, Kerouac made his rounds nonchalantly. In the office was a typewriter he could use two nights a week, a change from the constant handwriting (correspondence, journal) he had been doing since he left New York in July. One night he couldn't use the typewriter and he wrote a lengthy letter to Neal Cassady: "I can hardly wait till this winter when we'll be in New York and we'll start a new phase in our lives." Kerouac raised the possibility of going in the "coat-selling" business, a questionable venture Cassady had been involved in with Ginsberg the previous year. Kerouac was eager for Cassady to write back with his own plans which would have to be hatched during the spare time away from Carolyn, LuAnne, and his job. Kerouac urged Cassady to keep on writing, an act that was hardly a possibility when Neal was barely managing to scratch out letters atop a cardboard box. Unmindful of Cassady's many responsibilities, Kerouac wanted him to continue his jaunts to the Denver Library and extract a hefty volume of Balzac to read.

The work, both in the barracks and on paper was "intense," he wrote Ed White. However, the work wasn't what he planned and, as the likelihood of returning to sea diminished, Kerouac began to consider returning home. In a letter to his sister, Kerouac expressed the intensity of his desire to return to sea. He thought of attending purser's school before embarking upon one of two ships, the SS *Pres. Polk* or the SS *Pres. Monroe*. The expected pay for such an occupation was attractive to Kerouac, $280 a month as well as a private stateroom that he could write in. Of equal attraction was the possibility of world travel, for the *Monroe* typically sailed to eastern ports of call like the state of Hawaii, China, Japan, and even through the Panama Canal bound for New York. None of it would come to pass. Kerouac told his sister that he would have to ship out to sea before becoming eligible to attend purser's school. Why he didn't remains a quandry, since that was the reason he came to California in the first place.

Sometimes, while on duty, Kerouac, Cru, and another guard named Paul went out into the hills and shot at pheasants that they always seemed to miss (even the ones that were six yards away from them). The weeks in Marin City, however, became increasingly lonely. Letters spun out in every direction across the country, confiding friendship to Allen Ginsberg, eager restlessness to Neal Cassady, repeated assurances to his sister Caroline to send "rent" money to his mother (which he faithfully did, an average of 75 percent of his pay), and then more letters to Cassady urging his correspondence and expressing his desire to expand his writing capabilities.

His faith in Neal Cassady's writing never diminished. Even in 1959, Kerouac exuberantly described his pure belief in his Dean Moriarty as a writer. When asked by Al Aronowitz why Cassady never wrote anything of substance, Kerouac explained, "He has written . . . beautifully! He has written better than I have. In my opinion he's the most intelligent man I've ever met in my life." Kerouac said that Cassady "taught me everything that I now do believe about anything that there may be to be believed about divinity."

In late September, Kerouac turned in his pistol and badge to return to the road. Second-guessing his impulse to go home, he designed an alternate route for travel. He had his 40,000-word "movie story" that he thought attractive enough for Hollywood movie agents hungry for new ideas. However, Kerouac had neither the technical skill nor the discipline to ever write a film-worthy screenplay, a drawback he shared with William Faulkner. He had some contacts in Los Angeles, including Lon McAllister, a friend of his sister Caroline, who had urged him (in July 1944) to drop his relationship with Edie Parker and pursue writing in California.

On September 25, Kerouac reassessed the screenplay and found it "fair to middling" and decided that he would not be "mad" if they showed no interest in it: "Writing for the screen is pure plot and dialogue, my best writing is descriptive, such as in novels," he wrote to his sister. To Neal Cassady, he wrote that Cassady should drive Burroughs and Huncke to New York and, if Kerouac timed it right, he could rendezvous with Cassady in Texas.

The time had come to leave Marin County. Kerouac was ready to bail, but not before climbing nearby Mount Tamalpais, as he'd vowed. Also before leaving, he accompanied Cru to a dinner with his stepfather, who had practiced medicine in Viennese hospitals, and his wife. Kerouac arrived at the hotel where Cru's stepfather was staying, after drinking in the saloons of San Francisco. When he arrived, he used his best French to greet the tall, wizened man who reminded him of Burroughs. More drinks were poured and, before long, Kerouac was drunk. His sodden behavior embarrassed Cru and, to make things worse, Allan Temko joined in with his attempts at biting humor. Nonetheless, in an effort to impress, Cru shelled out his hard-earned cash for an evening at a fine restaurant. Cru warned Dianne and Jack to be in their best behavior: "There were times," Kerouac writes in *On the Road*, "when Remi was really the most gentlemanly person in the world," a sentiment shared by Edie Parker. Not eager for confrontation, he slipped out of Cru's place before they woke up.

It was a bad ending to a dubious start for Kerouac, but his recollections of his time there, plus the newest stockpile of ideas and thoughts, would ultimately weave themselves into a synthesis of road experiences for his new novel in progress.

THE MEXICAN GIRL

On October 14, Kerouac arrived in Oakland, bound for Los Angeles. He found that the city had the most interesting skid row in America. There were winos sunning themselves in front of a saloon and in front of the county jailhouse across the street. Railroad tracks crossed back and forth by old warehouses. Purveyors of tortillas and enchiladas cooked spiced meats and beans on Mexican carts seemingly on every corner. Men garbed in mackinaws and ranch hats reminded Kerouac of characters out of a Jack London story.

Two hundred and ninety-one miles south of Oakland, coasting along the San Joaquin Valley, Kerouac reached Bakersfield. At first, he attempted to hitchhike, walking as he thumbed through the valley "rich and dark at dusk" with the scents of grapes and melons wafting from pastures. The over-brimming sweetness of fig trees with tints from lemon trees created a synthesis of pleasure as he thumbed along the roadway. It was a virtual paradise, he found, befitting the people that worked the land; Mexican migrants whom worked at low wages without any expectations beyond their meager pay. Mexican women, he noted, had bodies ripened to perfection, as sweet looking as fat grapes and possessing, he naively imagined, "sweet, simple souls." The scenery reminded him of the stories of William Saroyan. Still, the cars, when they came, did not stop. They "rushed by, LA-bound. I gestured frantically," he remembers in *On the Road.* As dusk gave way to night, and then to midnight, the temperature plummeted. Resigned to purchasing another bus ticket, Kerouac walked back "shuddering" in a three-dollar army raincoat he bought for his travels to the Bakersfield bus station. Before boarding, he saw a Mexican girl "cutting across my sight":

> Her breasts stuck out straight; her little thighs looked delicious; her hair was long and lustrous black; and her eyes were great blue windows with timidities inside. I wished I were on her bus. A pain stabbed my heart, as it did every time I saw a girl I loved who was going the opposite direction in this too-big world.

Hopeful of a conquest (perhaps like Cassady's journey back to Denver from New York), he sat across from her. She was a

Mexican immigrant named Bea Franco and his companionship with her would ultimately become a hallmark of Part I in *On the Road*. Her pseudonym in the novel is "Terry."

The bus rocked through the unseasonably cool California night. Kerouac struck up a conversation with Bea, which she managed to maintain despite her broken English. She saw him as a WASP-ish, blue-eyed college boy, with his dark hair and pouting lip. Before long, he moved to sit with her. He found that she, too, was going to Los Angeles. Kerouac's attraction to her was genuine. He adored her petite frame, her seeming purity, and that she exemplified a race of people instilled with Catholic sanctity and tragedy. In *On the Road,* Kerouac saw a Spanish girl like her working a roadside stand possessing the "face of Jesus."

He disembarked the bus with her and soon found out she had a child, and a husband in Sabinal who abused her. She was going to Los Angeles to live with her sister until she could straighten her life out. Her son was now with her family, who picked grapes for a living in wine country. Kerouac told her that he was from New York, and she expressed her desire to move east as well. Kerouac, with amusement, told her she was free to move there with him anytime. He thought, "You could have all your Peaches and Bettys and Marylous and Ritas and Camilles and Inezes in this world." Her dark skin and her sense of relative purity attracted Kerouac more than the American girls he was used to. She was, he recalled in *On the Road,* his kind of "girlsoul."

As the bus pulled into Hollywood, Kerouac watched Tinsel Town pass before him. This was his destination, that "raged promised land," on which he planned a full-frontal assault armed only with his fresh screenplay. However, at the moment, he had a woman in his lap and some sort of mutual bond had developed between them. Disembarking on Hollywood's Main Street, the pair walked along the street. The bus depot held the beatest characters he could ever summon in a work of fiction. Here was the "mood" he sought for in his work, if he only knew how to capture it (which he did in his journal). He saw a "broken-down representative of God" preaching in one corner, a poor black preacher who appeared "seedy" to Kerouac.

"Bearded prospector hoboes" populated South Main Street. The squat buildings were redbrick, food smells drifted by, sometimes concealing the "whorey smell" of urbania. Urban offal, much like in the textile city in which he was raised and in New York City, took hold of his senses and before long, the momentary idyll began to fade. All at once, he suspected Bea Franco of being a hustler who worked the bus stations seeking to bilk naive tourists of their dollars. Somewhere, in the shadows, he felt her pimp was lurking. From the hotel window, as the hotel sign blinked its red neon on his drawn tired face, Kerouac watched the street as Bea slept. He saw cops arresting a man, heard the constant whining of the police sirens and the groan of the city.

Kerouac watched Bea, increasingly certain that she was a

whore. Seeking to soothe his rattling nerves, he ran out to purchase a bottle of whiskey. When he came back, he began to tell her about his New York friends. She became enraged when he brought up Vicki Russell, insisting to know more about the "six-foot redhead." She, in turn, began to suspect Kerouac of being a pimp. After convincing each other that they were both being straight with each other, they again enjoyed each other's company.

The next day, Kerouac planned in earnest to take Bea to New York. To accomplish this, it was necessary to earn some more money. Scanning the newspapers for jobs, Kerouac was also informed of the news of America. The newspaper informed them that a new wave of war dead had arrived on American shores. On October 27, 1947, a wartime Liberty ship, the SS *Joseph V. Connolly,* an army transport ship en route from Antwerp, Belgium, reached New York Harbor with its grim cargo of 6,248 dead GIs. Festooned with evergreens, sailors at attention along the port and starboard sides, and graced with a single flag-draped coffin on its bow containing a Medal of Honor recipient, the vessel moored. The thunder of the ship's guns boomed its salute through the narrow canyons of Manhattan, the New Jersey Palisades, and the lonely living room where Gabrielle sat waiting for her son to come home.*

* Less than a year later, SS *Joseph V. Connolly* caught fire 900 miles out in the North Atlantic and sank, becoming no more than a footnote in the pages of American history.

"THE MOST BRUTAL OF AMERICAN CITIES"

Los Angeles, the "city of angels," did not seem any different from New York City. "LA," he wrote in *On the Road,* lifted intact from his journal, "is the loneliest and most brutal of American cities." On the same day the *Connolly* pulled into port, a car veered off a Los Angeles road, hitting a tree. Three people were killed. Among them was a twenty-two-year-old wartime widow named Andrea M. Hernandez, anxiously waiting for her dead husband to be returned to her on the SS *Joseph V. Connolly.* Some days earlier, Louis William Rains was ruled insane and was committed to Mendocino State Hospital by a superior judge. When he believed that his live-in elderly aunt was trying to poison him, Rains beat her so badly that she died. On October 12, 1947, Sheppard W. King, a twenty-year-old father of a two-year-old boy, became incensed when the toddler spoke out loud inside a motion picture theater. Bringing his boy out to the lobby, King beat him until blood spurted from his nose. In a Hollywood jail, Sheppard denied abusing his son who was, at the moment, being treated at the Georgia Street Receiving Hospital for two black eyes, bruises to his head, and a cut lip.

Crimes, abuse, and bloodshed were an everyday reality in the western Promised Land, and searing headlines littered the paper Kerouac perused looking for a job. The streets of Los Angeles were dirty and crawling with vagrants. Cops were frisking people at will and the nightlife resembled nothing less than the lurid noir films that were in vogue.

Occasionally, the smell of marijuana drifted through the air, intermittently coiling with wisps of spicy chili. Kerouac could hear West Coast bebop. He was amazed by the large and varied assortment of people drifting from other parts of the country. Packrats, dusty and hungry, staggered in from the desert. There were homeless GIs who had yet to right themselves after being thrown into the horrible despair of war. On street corners, jaded prostitutes stood in "barely there" clothing. Most obvious, to Kerouac, were the broken-down hipsters who, like him, had wandered across the raw byways of America. He assembled from these sordid and squalid details material he explored more fully in later works.

Initially, Kerouac listed them in his notebook under "Themes for Stories." Some items were more simple than others: a cooling plate of untouched food lying on an abandoned plate; a woman telling a tale of her broken man, imbuing him with dignity; a bewhiskered boxcar hobo eating from a cold can of beef stew, whom Kerouac imagined wondering about the fate of Katharine Hepburn and Cary Grant after they departed for Europe in the film *Holiday.* He toyed again with a tentative ending for *The Town and the City* that would have the sense of departure. Peter, he felt, could plan a career as a purser in the merchant marines, perhaps reading "everything" and going "everywhere," much like his creator.

At Sunset and Vine, unemployed vagrants futilely applied for work at a drugstore. Others tried diners and drive-ins, in vain. With amusement, Kerouac noted the tourists searching for movie stars, shielding their eyes to glance into every shaded limousine that pulled over curbside. He sensed in the city a viper's pit of desperation and saw it, as others did, as the "boulevard of broken dreams." Young girls hoping to become Hollywood starlets ended up settling for work in soda fountains or exploited by unscrupulous opportunists promising them their "big break."

Kerouac opted for another bus ticket to take him and Bea Franco away from the city. They worked together to raise cash for further travels. Kerouac labored beside her picking grapes and cotton. The earthy romanticism he attached to such work in his later writings didn't match the reality of kneeling for hour upon hour of back-breaking labor. His hands were chafed raw and his fingertips bled. By early evening, the land grew cold and dark. Bea tended to stay with her child in a rented tent. Moneyless and despondent from hunger and the incessant chill in the air, she frantically wrote a note on a page of Kerouac's journal. She was considering taking her son and leaving with her brother Alex, who was coming to visit later that day: "It's so cold here for us. And we can't make anything picking Cotton." Kerouac, only capable of tolerating so much abject poverty, figured fifteen days with an indigent woman was all he could stand. Responsibility for others was not his forte, and gathering his gear, he told Bea that he would wait for her in New York if she ever chose to come. Handing him a photograph of herself, she perhaps did not hold out much hope that this would ever happen. The two parted, she one of dozens of women victimized by Kerouac's indecisiveness and lack of commitment.

RETURNING HOME

Kerouac's intention to meet Cassady in Texas would not be fulfilled. Cassady, Burroughs, and Huncke departed Texas in the last week of September on a Monday night, arriving in New York City four days later. Following them via train was Joan Vollmer Burroughs, who was strung out on Benzedrine. When she reached New York City, such was her impaired condition that she was promptly admitted to Bellevue. Though Cassady was responsible for chauffeuring everybody around in a car (including Vicki Russell, who he had the pleasure of "balling") his objective was only half as perilous as Burroughs's. He was trying to sell his cash crop to dealers around Manhattan. Cassady sent a letter from New York in early October reminding Kerouac that, besides Allen Ginsberg, "you're the only guy [. . .] I give a damn about, understand?" Neal stayed in New York for several weeks and departed only two days before Kerouac's arrival. Cassady returned to San Francisco by November 1947.

After leaving Bea Franco, Kerouac first went back to Los Angeles to pick up his unread film script from Columbia Pictures. The bus went through Albuquerque, New Mexico, and

Kansas City, Kansas, before pointing dead east for New York. He arrived on October 29, deep in "genuine surprise" recognizing that he was once again dropped into a past and a home, a mother, friends, clothes, food, and shelter. He felt himself to be a different person from the "boy" he had been before leaving New York. The novel, now just so many scattered pages on a desk, was the labor of "some other stranger." He was rested, despite feeling older than his age, and "much too world-wise to know anything right now."

Starved, he emptied the icebox, eating all he could handle. The refrigerator was brand new, purchased from Jack's California earnings. After Gabrielle retired to her bed, Jack lay in his own, still restless and overtired from his journey. Only two days previous, Neal slept in his bed waiting for Jack to arrive; he could wait no longer and returned west. Kerouac recollected this time in his April 1951 draft of *On the Road*: "I never dreamed that first night at home I would see Neal again and that it would start over again, the road, the whirlwind road, more than in my wildest imaginings foresaw."

CHAPTER THREE

BACK HOME

Kerouac was geared to leap back into the "humility and decency of writing," resuming his log to map the slow, laborious process of completing *The Town and the City.* The beginning of November was like toeing cold water before the leap in. Scribbling some notes about its constant difficulty, he began in earnest at five o'clock the evening of November 3.

The feeling of, and need for, the road had not shaken off yet. Kerouac right away speculated about another road trip, this time a northwest trek to Canada with Hal Chase, the archetypal "sincere, intense guest" that he required as company. But *The Town and the City* needed completion if he was to justify himself as a writer at all. The past seven years had been largely composed of inspired fits and starts and abandoned novels. Those works originally designed to be novels instead shriveled to novellas or mere character sketches. They were, in his rash estimate (and wrongly, for there are many fine pieces buried in the wealth of his notebooks and reams of typescript) "just no good."

The first week home, he eked out a few stops and starts. Then, all at once, the words urged themselves forth in an inspired surge. It was liberating to finally spill out his new ideas into the vast sweep of his family saga. On Friday the seventh, he composed 2,500 words in only a few hours. That evening brought him 1,500 more: "Not that it's easier, it's only *more myself*." He sensed "mastery" and recognized that such inspired confidence had been denied to him for "my long mournful years of work, blind powerful work." He was blinded no longer. His vision was sharp, delivering the sweep of his saga in seemingly effortless passion. He had the foresight not to bog himself down with vivid descriptive detail, but instead to knife the edge of his prose with "narrative power."

By the second week of November, his confidence began to lag, and he became prone to bouts of self-effacing rambling in his journal. Dismissing his paranoia as "French Canadian . . . gaucheries," he forged ahead determinedly: 2,500 words a session on average, 4,000 a day while hacking away at the troubling vines of ennui and self-doubt. His goal was 15,000 words a week, which would guarantee completion by early the next year.

To keep himself on track, Kerouac gave himself pep talks in his journal, rallying about the benefits of "self-knowledge," when the "sublime child in us is stilled and in its place has come a sallow maturity." This in fact is the fallacy of adulthood, for this maturity can defeat an artist if it measures the world in mathematical precision, every calculation measured precisely without room for instinct or inspiration. It was a "gloomy" prospect, for he felt that such an outlook could hamper the new work that he began to toy with.

On the Road was to be different than the deliberate labors of *The Town and the City*. The road novel would require him to capture the "half-animal" peripatetic nature of his existence trekking across the continent. Kerouac's eagerness to resume a "full human life" at Ozone Park was undermined by the effects of the road. "I find it hard to return to something essential and devout in my feeling for life and after a long siege of raw vagabondage." "The word "vagabondage" had associations to him of slavery and bestial necessity. The road had taught him that humanity will perish when faced with exhaustion, bodily defeat, and neglect. It had allowed him to measure his vulnerability, to see that the chances of his survival were "frail and catastrophic" in the rawness of the land around him. Kerouac recognized that only three things were required for existence: endurance, patience, and alertness.

The new ideas threatened to derail the "two years effort" invested into *The Town and the City.* They arose in early December. "I decided to resume and finish Town & City before anything else. This was my physical system itself, the man itself, revolting against any abandonment of two years of supreme effort, since after all this new idea is not new, and all the magnificent structures of T & C were dedicated laboriously, painfully and patiently to the same end—proof of that is Peter Martin's absorption with 'the world itself' in T & C, and other things." Further efforts to this end were later manifested in varying plot structures and character developments in *On the Road*.

Kerouac's attraction to women, though as urgent as ever, was tempered by his false sense of maturity. When he followed two girls down the street, he stopped himself, knowing that "different laws existed for me." In the long run, he imagined, having one woman, a wife that would make all the difference in the world for him. He felt he would probably end up chasing the next girl he saw, but turning away from those two was an act of real "sincerity"—realizing that he could measure himself by his true accomplishments and not simple conquest of the female heart. Kerouac chose for distraction a girl he nicknamed "Dark Eyes," who visited him in Ozone Park. Sometimes they spent time dancing in the living room, or sitting on the handmade rug Gabrielle had woven, as she looked on at her son probably hopeful that this time he would settle down with a "nice" girl.

The ideas, constant and urgent, roiled inside him. He sensed himself as a young man capable of falling into the "throes of the criminal lassitudes of heart." The world, spiraling in a never-ending cycle of disorder, was something he was beginning to understand instead of being caught up within. He intuited that other people were not interested in extracting themselves from this "lassitude." They did not want simple "salvation through gratitude and joy." He recognized, by knowing himself, how others could fall into a trap of "melancholy habits." Empathetically, he felt the sadness of the world. In the news that week, Kerouac read of suicides and child murderers, and sensed that madness that brought such misery and annihilation into the world was the by-product of "empty chaotic hearts" and the "sleepy, fretful annoyance of the sick, the irritated, the asleep." In a way, he felt himself capable of doing the same, had he not been able to harness his own guilts and depression in his work.

Kerouac's choices of reading material during the waning days of 1947 were Dostoevsky's *A Raw Youth* and Stendahl's *Le Rouge et le Noir.* Despite his choice of dark material, he would not allow it to influence his writing, acknowledging that there was too much of the "pale criminal" with us, and not enough simple beauty. The idea was to choose the "center of existence," like that of the wedding between Princess Elizabeth and Prince Philip that month, an event of mass adoration that Kerouac for the moment concurred with, preferring that festivity to the "daemonic relationships of neurotics and fools" he had been exposed to in Denver, New York City, and with Ginsberg and Cassady.

During Thanksgiving, after a dinner of roast duck, Kerouac continued his reading of *A Raw Youth* and *The Life of Goethe.* He was attracted to the Faust legend, which he used later in *Doctor Sax.* Goethe's colorful descriptions of the Italian landscape in *Italian Journey* inspired him to similar themes during the composition of *On the Road.* After dinner, Kerouac had a long "gossipy" conversation with his mother. A willing student, he listened as she pontificated on the "fat, happy Russian women" and the consequences of communism in Russia. She felt that "Russia might yet be saved when *the women bring the men down to their knees*." When Kerouac repeated Gabrielle's opinion of Russia to Joan Burroughs, and that she felt a "man is not a man if he doesn't respect women," Joan wryly responded that it "sounded like a veiled threat of castration."

Kerouac was hesitant to warm up to his Columbia pals, and sensed that he was just as prone to pessimism as they were. On November 22, arguing with Burroughs and Ginsberg about the merits of psychoanalysis and "horror," he felt they were "still wrapped up in the same subjects over the past two years": distinctly , it was their tendency to become eerie parallels of Dostoevsky characters. To the Russian master's credit, it was his ability to create characters of extreme psychological depth making it possible for Kerouac and his compatriots to apply aspects of his work to themselves. From the pale, saintlike Prince Myshkin of *The Idiot,* the sensual Dmitri Karamazov and his mystical brother Aloysha, to the existentialist Underground Man of *Notes from the Underground,* each was characterized by bitterness and isolation—each of these and others correlate the shifting moods of the Beat writers.

However, Kerouac wished to shake off such borrowed personae and, instead, delve deeper into himself. Now that his experiences were broader, everything else seemed to pale in significance to the yawning stretch of the American West. He was nonetheless drawn to his friends. Throughout the winter of 1947/48, he was with Burroughs and Ginsberg constantly, trying out snatches of his newly typed prose on them, eager for approval and defensive at criticism.

Kerouac was leery of book critics at this time, an attitude that increased when he began publishing novels. Reading criticism of Dostoevsky's *The Brothers Karamazov* and *The Raw Youth* (which he had finished reading by the first week of December), he found that American critics were socially ignorant and did not understand the "facts of life." Americans, in his estimation, were content to remain buried within the gritty layers of their "emotional makeups," which was exclusive to the United States.

Despite Kerouac's reservations about Ginsberg's attachment to Neal Cassady, a conversation with him on December 5 revealed to each the similarities of their perceptions.

Kerouac sensed Ginsberg's seriousness beneath his facade of being "clever." The chief difference, Kerouac detected, between himself and Ginsberg was that the latter always seemed to have a sense of "space" about him, a "mysteriously incomprehensible" vastness that threatened to overwhelm him. Kerouac, on the contrary, was always aware of his surroundings, a strength that contributed to the richness of his mature prose. The other difference Kerouac sensed was that Ginsberg's vision of life was "deeper," culminating in the idea that life, in its purest essence, was only a comedy. Kerouac, in contrast, possessed more gravity, more seriousness: "My vision emphasizes the urge to brooding self-envelopment while all the love is going on, that is, people have to work and live while they love." Lastly, Kerouac felt that Ginsberg's vision was more "beautiful" and "benign," a sweetness that he felt to be genuine. Kerouac's conversation with Ginsberg made his ulterior motives all too clear, and it inspired him to begin a new work, a novel, from which he sketched a fledgling idea and tucked it away for later.

Ginsberg's material for his poetry had become more dramatic and life changing. He dispensed with the archaic language that peppered the "Denver Doldrums" and "Dakar Doldrums"—"thy," "thou," "thee" and the like—but still toed the line of an A-B-A-B rhyme scheme (with some slight variations). Through 1948 and 1949, Ginsberg incorporated into his poems snippets of Kerouac's dreams, prose, and ideas until he took Jack's advice and reinvented his creative strategy. Kerouac suggested that the true gems of his poetry lie in his journals in raw, unadulterated form. It would take a few more years for Ginsberg to realize this and, once he did, it would reshape his poetry for the rest of his life.

On November 14, 1947, Dr. Harry J. Worthing, the senior director of the Pilgrim State Hospital, sent Ginsberg a form to authorize a prefrontal lobotomy for his mother, Naomi. Louis and Naomi had divorced, leaving their son responsible for this dramatic decision. Ginsberg authorized the surgery. After the operation was performed, he punished himself with guilt that remained with him for the rest of his life. This event would find its poetic apex in "Kaddish," published in 1958: "O mother / what have I left out" . . . " with your eyes of shock / with your eyes of lobotomy;" . . . "farewell / with Communist party and a broken stocking."

The close of the year yielded remarkable progress for a two-month span of time. Kerouac rarely left Ozone Park to go into the city. When he grew lonesome, he wrote letters to Ginsberg asking him why he wasn't answering his phone ("I've called you at your W. 27th place at least 20 times, or a dollar's worth of phone calls, and almost every time your landlady hung up on me in disgust, as though she were mad because you receive so many calls" (JK to Ginsberg, January 2, 1948). Work on the "Greenland" section of chapter 10 of part 2 of *The Town and the City* was suspended for a week. Before quitting it, Kerouac referred to his sea diary of 1942 to elicit the "Melvillean" passages he felt would be useful.

Plans were afoot for him and his mother to go to North Carolina to visit Nin and Paul Blake for the Christmas holiday.

Paranoid Kerouac harbored a temporary change of heart toward Cassady, who was still corresponding with Ginsberg. To Ginsberg, he wrote, "It seems to me that both you and Neal are making yourselves obnoxious with your condescending attitudes toward the rest of us." Kerouac was also taken aback by Cassady's seeming indifference toward a fragment of his novel that he had retyped for him.

More to Kerouac's liking was Cassady's statement that he had begun writing in earnest, both a personal journal and an account of his early life, a feat made more impressive by the fact that he was still seeing two women at the same time. Though Cassady managed to "extract an annulment" from LuAnne, he still enjoyed her physically. To Kerouac, Cassady wrote, "Aside from the emotional difficulty there is another and, I feel, more interesting problem—i.e. keeping Lu and Carolyn separated. This game has been going on for a month and is exciting in many ways. I am with both of them at different hours of the same day, daily, I must be on my toes to keep Carolyn from knowing." In Kerouac's mind, Cassady was building up a character he had in mind for *On the Road.*

THE TOWN AND THE CITY

The Town and the City, in Kerouac's estimate, was now only a month and a half from completion. Despite feeling that the world was against him, he was in high spirits. The novel was now a "monstrous edifice" Kerouac now felt chained with. Looking over the fat manuscript, he saw two chaotic fragments written by a young man blinded by zeal and optimism: "Somewhere I took the wrong road and I did it earnestly and with furious energy, in great irretrievable labours." His new ideas for a book peeled away luscious slices of humanity in lieu of naturalistic prose writing.

But by January 11, Kerouac was passionate about completing *The Town and the City.* A visit by Ginsberg interrupted a furious spurt of 2,500 words that was completed at four o'clock in the morning. (Ginsberg wanted to tell Kerouac that he felt he was going "mad" and was on the verge of throwing a "fit" [or so Kerouac felt]). On Valentine's Day, Ginsberg confided to his journal that he was still madly amorous of Cassady: "O Neal I love you still and I wish you were here, yet you become more lost each day; you are most near while I do not even hear from you or send you news to me" (Ginsberg, journal entry February 14, 1948). Kerouac calmed Ginsberg by reading from his large, unwieldy manuscript that now needed a box as deep as a shoe box to contain it. In all likelihood, he read the more poetic passages, the "wild echoing misty March night," the "moon meadows" of the highway, or Mickey Martin's "absorbed morning frown"; or maybe the larger-than-life play-by-play motions of high school football captured so beautifully from Kerouac's own youth, how the fifes and "muffled drums dolorously beat out the doom of certain hopes and certain destiny."

Ginsberg's assessment was that it seemed "greater than Melville" and that it had a shot at being the next "great American novel." Ginsberg relayed that enthusiasm to Cassady via letter: "What finally pulled me out—to name an external cause since they are the signs by which we mark seasons—was Jack's novel. It is very great, beyond my wildest expectations. I never knew." Nor did many others who, though they may have accepted his commitment, never imagined his remarkable understanding of the human condition.

Though it was a great compliment, Kerouac realized that Ginsberg could never truly "see him." At times, Ginsberg spent as much as thirty hours drinking, reading, and discussing the intricacies of craft with him. However, if Kerouac wanted an honest assessment of his work, he would have to discard the mask he wore in the presence of Ginsberg: "Right now I think of him exactly as he thinks of himself." Ginsberg was, in the words of Kerouac in January 1948, a man who "giggles" at the rest of the world, "except his own horror." Kerouac likened him to a wooden-faced grinning gargoyle affixed to the prow of a great ship that "crosses southern seas, passes icebergs and albatrosses, noses into grimy old harbors, stands anchored in flowery lagoons, weathers bright sunshine, gray fog, great storms, blackest night, and finally sinks to the bottom of the ocean, where, amid bubbling muds and weird fishes and sea-light, the gargoyle-head still grins and giggles forever."

At *The Town and the City*'s first anniversary on January 17, 1948, exactly a year since its beginning in earnest, it was 225,000 words, with 50,000 left to go. The brunt of the early work, when he looked back, was completed in March 1946, spurred by his desire to impress Cassady. His goal was to complete the novel before his twenty-sixth birthday on March 12, but there were complications. It was not the novel he had mapped out in his head, but it was the "best he could do" and he remained satisfied. He had to justify his aesthetic; that what he wrote was the creative output of a "sane" writer as opposed to the "psychotic sloppiness" of Joyce (who he admired and was heavily indebted to early in his writing career).

Cassady's own writing, like Kerouac's, sought to express the inexpressible. In his words, he sought to grope toward the "personal." "There is something there that wants to come out; something of my own that must be said." Beneath this drive was self-doubt, "perhaps words are not for me." Cassady felt that the writing process should eliminate all rules, conventions, or feeble attempts at forging a writing style. The vocabulary should remain simplified, with "lordly clauses and phrases" eliminated if at all possible. Instead, a writer should savor each word like a precious swallow of port: "I think, one should write, as nearly as possible, as if he were the first person on earth and was humbly and sincerely putting on paper that which he saw and experienced, loved and lost; what his passing thoughts were and his sorrows and desires [. . . .]" A true example of this, he felt, would be to concoct a potent synthesis of Thomas Wolfe, Gustave Flaubert, and Charles Dickens. Cassady elaborated in his letter to Kerouac in January 1948 that the best art was that which sprang from "necessity." Keeping that in mind, he assured his friend that he would nonetheless keep "grinding out the trash" that was still "embedded" in him.

During the month of February, Kerouac tried a different approach to energize his sluggish attitude toward completing the novel: physical and mental conditioning. He walked two miles a day after he finished writing and before he went to sleep, punctuated by sets of pull-ups. Drinking had, of late, soured his mood, for he frequently woke up with hang-overs thus putting a damper on his writing. His sleep was filled with "nervous dreams" and sometimes when he woke, he did not know who he was. He attended the theater in Times Square and, once again, began reading books on American history and geography. To reward himself after completing the "city" section of his novel, Kerouac began reading Mark Twain, who was one of his literary heroes.

Kerouac's birthday came and went with completion nowhere near. On March 22, he completed the "city" half of the novel. The novel was finally completed after a furious three months of retyping former sections and creating newer sequences to bridge the "town" with the "city" sections of the book. Some of passages, concerning the Merrimack River or "glee," would be subsequently cut by his later editor, Robert Giroux. Other times, Kerouac toyed with handwritten passages, revising them over and over again before considering placement into the typewritten manuscript. "I want to be a significant writer and I also want to live in a vast and significant way, like Twain almost. That's my present feeling, no Faustian torments that swirl futile and self-destructive around oneself, but a life that reaches out to others like two arms."

He plotted out the remainder of the novel, including the section concerning Francis Martin, the funeral of the father, and the concluding chapters. The end was now in sight. He sketched out ideas on pieces of paper, outlines for a new novel that would incorporate American ideals drawn from Mark Twain, and the rereading of the "simplicity, humbleness and beauty" of *Look Homeward, Angel.*

Drama with Ginsberg reached a new low when the struggling poet begged Kerouac to hit him in the face. Kerouac rejected the idea, and wrote in his journal that it was the "end as far as I'm concerned." Unconsciously, he harbored a desire to hurt Ginsberg, but his loving and respectful friendship for the man prompted him to half-heartedly explain his way out of a personal issue Ginsberg had taken offense to. Kerouac's assessment of the moment was that it resembled the folly of their youths, that it was "90% false and 10% childish." Subsequently, he reduced Ginsberg and his ilk to "unimportant neurotics." "I go to see them in a happy, fond frame of mind and always come away baffled and disgusted. *This does not happen among my other friends* [meaning Ed White, Tom Livornese, Hal Chase, etc.], therefore I should heed my feelings in these matters and stick to birds of my own feather."

However, "birds of his own feather," if he assessed himself objectively, meant an obsessed self-absorbed egocentric who seldom had time for others when in lockdown on a work at hand. Quite accurately, Kerouac realized his "insane human pride," but it was always undermined by a constant current of self-doubt. His ideal of "universal sympathy" had no real place but in his writing: "Such things are for idiots, hypocrites, and mad charlatans of the soul." He continued, more determined than ever, to justify his innate selfishness, "I will recognize that I'm human and must limit my sympathies, my *active* sympathies, to the life I have and will have, and that any other course is not true. I have been a fool and a liar and a shifty weakling by pretending that I was the friend of these people—Ginsberg, Joan, Carr, Burroughs, [David] Kammerer even, some others—when all the time I must have known that we all naturally disliked each other and were just grimacing incessantly in a comedy of malice." Of them all, Kerouac deemed himself the most "furtive" of the lot.

On the Denver home front, Cassady's involvement with Carolyn and LuAnne became so extreme that it began to affect him physically. He broke out in hives and his throat swelled, impairing his respiratory tract. His hand was also in pain, which he was prescribed medication for (also to control his breakout of hives). Neal now owned a twenty-year-old Chevy purchased for $225. Despite his new wheels, he was grounded in Denver by his domestic responsibilities. He did not write Kerouac again for six months.

Neal Cassady still wrought from the drama of his life a continuous streak of semi-autobiographical writing replete with harshly applied exaggeration and sheer bullshit. His commitment, however, faltered at the obstacles he faced regarding style and continuity in his craft. He found himself "looking to others for the answer to my soul," a futile gesture in the face of the opaque one-dimensional indifference of many of his contemporaries toward him. His answer, a good one, was to seek further assistance from Kerouac and Ginsberg. Like Kerouac, he faced the specter of self-doubt: "I am not too sure that the roots of the impulse to write go deep enough, are necessary enough, for me to create on paper," he confided to Kerouac on January 7, 1948.

A WESTERN RANCH

Kerouac once again turned his attention to the idea of building a ranch in the west. On a rainy day in May, he wrote to Neal Cassady. He reminded Cassady of the early days when he first came to New York City with LuAnne, when he was in the early stages of wrestling with his novel. It was Cassady's urgent prompting that pushed Kerouac to completion: "I went on blasting away at it just to impress and more to please you." *The Town and the City*'s turning point was at that moment he confided to Cassady: "What an amazing thing to realize that you, more than anyone else, can be said to be the biggest pitchfork that got me howling and screaming across the pea-patch towards my inevitable duties. It's that wonderful Nealish creativeness that did it." Then Kerouac placed Cassady amongst the wide and varied stable of friends and acquaintances: "Others may criticize, others may hurt me, others may suggest darkly, others may not care, others may watch without emotion—but you yell and gab away and fill me with a thousand reasons for writing and getting a big story done. And to think that you haven't been back to glance at it? Why didn't you read some of it when you were waiting for me last October!" The novel had one remaining chapter, that of Peter Martin's departure into the darkness and uncertainty of the lonely road (JK to NC, May 7, 1948).

Kerouac's progress, he wrote in his journal, was impeded by his excitement about owning a ranch and the "subject of cattle raising." First, he pondered soliciting a Lowell friend he had known since his boyhood, Mike Fournier, who was living penniless on a farm in Massachusetts, trying to raise five children. The other possibility was his brother-in-law, Paul Blake Sr. But both were too preoccupied with keeping their families housed and fed. Cassady was the key. Living with Cassady and working on a ranch would free Kerouac from all of his East Coast ties. Kerouac, naively assuming that learning about it in "books" would equip him for the rigors of ranching, assured Cassady that he was ready for it. His immediate plan was to begin the next summer, to work on various ranches throughout Colorado, Arizona, and Wyoming. All they would need would be three hundred head of cattle, a "spread" of alfalfa to feed them with, and a crop of vegetables for food. He realized that he would never make enough money from his book to buy all that, but he was willing to rent or lease it, as long as he could "live a good life in the canyon countries, lots of forage, trees, high sharp mountain air . . . and marry a Western girl and have six kids." Though he felt it all to be but a dream, he reminded Cassady that his new novel had also once been a dream, it was ultimately finished because "you were around to prod me." Cassady, however, did not respond to Kerouac's letters due to the new domestic difficulties and his downward spiral into debauchery.

In June, Kerouac excitedly informed Allen Ginsberg that he had finally heard from Cassady, who was in the unforgivingly hot desert of Pixley, California: "[E]ach time I'd start a reply I'd have to quit, either because it became a foolish lovenote & plea for your sympathy, help, understanding & forgiveness, or because in describing any tortures I'd become too overbalanced or too distastefully, incoherently mad" (Cassady to JK, June 16, 1948). Cassady's last six months had been filled with misadventures. He bought a 1941 Packard club coupe and, after racing it 14,000 miles across America for 85 days (an exaggeration to impress the gullible Kerouac), returned it unpaid for. Suicidal impulses urged him to drive through stop signs hoping that he would get "hit." For his birthday, Cassady stole a .38 caliber revolver and held it to his temple several times over the span of fourteen hours but was unable to pull the trigger. He then drove across the continental divide without snow chains or antifreeze, hoping to freeze himself to death. Again he backed away from his suicidal impulse by flagging down a bus to push his car out of the snow.

Cassady then returned to San Francisco, having caught a case of the crabs from a young girl he met along the way. He explained to Kerouac that he drove her from Greeley to San Francisco, where he deserted her in a hotel room. Two weeks later, he picked her up and brought her to Sacramento "to a whorehouse & she's there now—whoring & eating cock—the bitch." A couple of weeks later, Cassady met up with a "young nigger boy" and his "30 yr old sugar mama." Cassady, if he didn't participate in their sexual relations, watched them go at it: "three times they do it—every other *hour*,—every day. I stay there & get high & dig great music." He found a girl to join him and proudly watched as she made it with the both of them before a debauched "4 way orgy" took place. His return to Denver to divorce LuAnne almost killed him when he fell asleep at the wheel after driving forty-six hours straight. On April 1, he married Carolyn. The next day, he began work on the Southern Pacific Railroad, but the job did not last because the railroad business was at a low financial ebb. Cassady applied for an ordinary seaman position for the marine division of the Standard Oil Company. Jobs lost followed jobs gained, each reflecting Cassady's inclination to transience. By the time he wrote to Kerouac, Carolyn was seven months pregnant with Neal's fifth child. His plan for the child, if it was a boy, was to name him after Jack and Allen: John Allen Cassady.

Remaining hopeful of populating his planned life on a ranch with a brood of little Kerouacs, Jack began projecting the women he met into his plans. When he met eighteen-year-old Beverly Gordon in May 1948, he saw in her the potential of achieving marital bliss. He followed her one day to a roller-skating rink and, watching her, pondered the imponderable: "She has all the amazing qualities of womanhood: a low voice, a statuesque figure, dark midnight eyes, moonlight skin—and youth, the grace of a little girl. And *consciousness.* And *sadness.* And *simplicity.* And finally, the one woman in whose eyes I see humility, not vanity. A proud and secret darkness surrounds her; just right for Colorado; just ripe for six babies." His attraction to her, he felt, reflected a "truer sense" of himself. However, his cheap dates and her suspicions about his not having a job elicited rejection. Believing that he had been wronged, Kerouac vented into his journal about his beliefs of a "classless" society and how she had no right to treat him the way that she did. His intentions of ranching and being a writer were of a nobler, loftier vein, one profoundly transcending such a petty and useless concept as "class."

Kerouac was beginning to find that he was exemplary at attracting women, but not at keeping them. Drawing inspiration from Abraham Lincoln's speech of December 1, 1862, he realized that companionship was the "last, best hope on earth," that it was the job of humanity to drive away the cold clutches of nature with warmth and love. To do so meant shedding the accelerating demands of modern living and opting for more old-fashioned ideals. On the bright side, Cassady was favorable toward Kerouac's idea. "Your ranching is beautiful," Cassady said, "if you're serious & want a man who will make $350 to $400 a month on the railroad every year from May to January—& his wife & his child & his knowledge of ranch work & his love for you & your mother—then, take me." Cassady had met Gabrielle Kerouac during his first visit to New York City and he was optimistic that she and Carolyn would "get along together famously." Cassady urged that they to live together on the ranch right away.

Ginsberg was less than enthused about Cassady's new marriage. His recent readings of Yeats, Blake, and Dostoevsky were colored by vivid dreams of Neal Cassady. Though his life was much improved (he maintained a regular income as a copy boy for the Associated Press), he was still obsessed by Cassady: "the idea of you with a child and a settled center of affection—shit." However, his life drastically changed when in July 1948, a series of visions of hearing William Blake's voice while lying in bed masturbating caused him to reassess his life as a poet. Already Kerouac's hard work on *The Town and the City* had impressed and inspired him. Now it was his time to take up the reins of creative discipline and forge a voice, a *true* voice of his own.

"STATEMENT OF SANITY"

When Kerouac wasn't musing on a penny on the floor of his Ozone Park apartment and pondering the meaningless of money in the world, he wrote insightful mini-essays into his notebook. He was realizing how he differed from other men who worked to reap an income from the unforgiving world they inhabited. "The modern thinking man, in his emphasis on despair, seems to have a knack for posing his own fears without challenging them." The fear of self-defeat was, by Kerouac's admission, their downfall. Only the creative types, the "thinking-man," craved defeat. In the years to come, defeat was a constant unwanted guest darkening Kerouac's doorway.

Comparing his own dilemma with that of Thomas Wolfe and Joseph Conrad, Kerouac wondered how *they* were able to accomplish what they did. But his alignment with Wolfe's selfish sensibilities began to shift when he was formulating his ideas to run a western ranch. "Why did Wolfe labor so prodigiously to *prove* that he had talent and meanwhile forgetting that he was a man, a human being with a life to live in the world." Writers like Mark Twain were able to write while being "true men in every sense." Twain's busy life on Mississippi steamboats, his roaming of the West, digging silver in Nevada mines, being a newspaper editor and a family man, contradicted the popular misconception of the lone artist having to slave away in his chamber. Thinking of Twain, Kerouac considered the possibility of working a ranch while forging a creative path as an author. Though he ardently admired the novels of Joseph Conrad and Thomas Wolfe, Kerouac thought them "terribly lonely and unhappy, unnatural men." Sacrificing life for art was "stupid nonsense"—the opposite of what he had felt only a couple of years before. He also discounted the "nonsense" of Arthur Rimbaud, Friedrich Nietzsche and André Gide. With this problem solved, Kerouac sought to apply to himself a new manifesto: "Let's have another man who lives his life in the world, complete, and also writes great books."

CHAPTER FOUR

"I Am a Hoodlum and a Saint"

By the close of 1948, Jack Kerouac was talking to God.

Kerouac often likened himself to his childhood model, Saint Thérèse of Lesieux: "Love proves itself by deeds, so how am I to show my love? Great deeds are forbidden me. The only way I can prove my love is by scattering flowers and these flowers are every little sacrifice, every glance and word, and the doing of the least actions for love." In his search for universal compassion, Kerouac also composed psalms and hymns as spiritual signposts that he was on the right path. Sometimes he became frustrated when he could not feel God; other times His presence instilled serenity and joy and, more importantly, inspiration. The "forge-fires" of creation burned like kindling in his heart and for this, he thanked God abundantly. This was committed by "direction" of the Lord, and, in Kerouac's words, he wholeheartedly embraced the process:

> Let me find You now, like new joy on the earth at morning, like a horse in his meadows in the morning seeing his master a-coming across the grass—Like steel, I am now, God, like steel, you have made me strong and hopeful.
>
> Strike me and I will ring like a bell!

In October 1948, Kerouac set his sights anew on the "road" novel, envisioning it as a book "dealing with hitch-hiking and the sorrows, hardships, adventures, sweats and labours of that." The premise of it was locked. The characters, "two boys," are on their way westward to California, each pursuing separate objectives. One doing so for the sake of his "girl," and the other, to pursue "Golden Hollywood or some such illusion." It was a dream chase, illustrating the vanity and futility of spending one's life in an endless struggle to wrangle from life an unobtainable American Dream. They were to be regular guys, working dead-end jobs in factories, carnivals, lunchcarts, and farms. That road, traveled with perseverance and stoic calm, ended on the distant West Coast, ultimately finding out that their determination was for naught.

Excited by the prospects of such a novel, Kerouac zealously wrote Hal Chase, "[T]hese ideas and plans obsess me so much that I can't conceal them." Likening himself to Goethe, he felt that his enthusiasm tended to "overflow out of me." At times accosting strangers in bars, Kerouac spilled out the breadth and depth of his new idea (JK to Hal Chase, October 19, 1948). This version of *On the Road,* one Kerouac later felt was an important work in itself, staggered along for ninety-five pages, all 40,000 words of it giving the impression of *leaning* toward *something* but nonetheless never achieving it. His "high pitched" motivation made him think he could finish *On the Road* by the next winter. To do so, he quit attending classes at the New School for Social Research paid for by the GI Bill.

During the autumn of 1948, Kerouac wrestled feverishly with the naturalistic *On the Road* and simultaneously with *Doctor Sax*'s more visionary prose style. He started on the latter three times before settling upon a beginning he was content with. Aiming at a more confessional tone in his writing, he also detected an insincerity in his voice (as he did whenever he was consumed by self-doubt). His recent classes with Professor Alfred Kazin at the New School for Social Research distracted him. Though he attended lectures given by dramatist Eugene O'Neill, his real motive was to continue writing on his own, apart from the demands of the New School's curriculum.

Despite the distractions, he gave himself only two months to complete *Sax*. On November 2, Kerouac was merging older material with new in order to have another manuscript to sell simultaneously with *The Town and the City*. Days later, he grew frustrated with *Doctor Sax* and began *On the Road*.

He had, of late, begun working out "new ideas" despite lacking a true feel for his work-in-progress. Six thousand words were rapidly committed to paper to "see how much a man can do." Again, his progress faltered when he was besieged by term papers and exams. With regret he put aside his work and began thinking of new ways to make his writer's block dissolve. Kerouac's feeling of "falseness" was brought on by his lack of the spiritual freedom he'd felt during *The Town and the City*'s composition. Part of his issues with the "real world" was his lack of faith in the will of society. This extended itself to the publishers he was courting at the moment. Anxiously awaiting word from Little, Brown, Kerouac vented his frustrations by taking long walks around Brooklyn. By doing so, he could lose himself in his thoughts, solve writing problems, and take in fresh sights and sounds. However, his perverse change of spirit saw him pondering "daydreams of destruction." In his mind he drew a gun from a holster and shot at oncoming cars. To others walking by, he imagined he wrapped his hands around their throats to choke them. Dark and brooding, he later compared himself to Kurtz in *Heart of Darkness,* wanting to "exterminate the brutes" with "complete honesty."

• • •

In the ensuing days, he forged ahead with his road novel with "mad new ideas" despite its tangled writing process. There were time shifts, new characters, and picaresque elements, all transmuted to present a fresher, more honest artistic sensibility. Specifically, he incorporated a central character named Ray Smith (later used as Kerouac's pseudonym in the novel *The Dharma Bums*), whose experiences resembled parts of his own life. Despite not knowing how the book would end, Kerouac still felt it moved along with a "greater freedom" than *The Town and the City.* In this furious run of writing, Kerouac accumulated 32,500 words between November 9 and 29.

His devotion to the novel was not without its risks. Because he was skipping most of his classes now, Kerouac risked losing much-needed government stipend money ($75 monthly). Yet his excitement outweighed financial jeopardy: "My new novel is growing in my mind" he confided to his journal. *On the Road,* he felt, was a sure bet for he felt it had appeal to everybody, unlike the mystical hallucination of *Doctor Sax.* Lowell buddy Mike Fournier told Kerouac that he should stick to writing "true action stories." In truth, Kerouac felt that the quality of his writing at the moment was poor and that what he was committing to paper was nothing more than experimental.

IAN MACARTHUR AND OTHERS

In December 1948, as Kerouac awaited word from Cassady, he was becoming closer to John Clellon Holmes (Ian MacArthur in *On the Road*), a man who refused to let "life slip out of his hands." Kerouac had first met Holmes in July 1948. He, like Kerouac, was a New Englander born in the small town of Holyoke, Massachusetts. The two shared similar sensibilities about life, philosophy, and art. On a regular basis, Kerouac shared with Holmes his journal as well as some pages of works-in-progress. In November 1948, he gave Holmes the manuscript of *Doctor Sax* and later, the manuscript of *On the Road.* Holmes's truthfulness and frank nature was of special value to Kerouac. At one point, for example, Holmes suggested that the character of Doctor Sax needed a more mythical underpinning to make it work. Holmes had a different view of *On the Road;* his positive reception, at least for the *idea* of the novel, bolstered Kerouac's vacillating confidence. Kerouac's composition of the novel had recently induced a trancelike state as he typed at rapid speed. Liberated and exuberant, he realized that this was greatest "break" in his writing since the previous fall after returning from California. It was as if he had been released from a "verbal-emotional prison."

Holmes was also observing the writer with his work. He felt that Kerouac often behaved immaturely, having seen him at parties and other social gatherings. Alcohol tended to turn the normally taciturn Kerouac into a state that was by turns boisterous and pouting. Holmes was not alone; New School professor Brom Weber and composer David Diamond, among others, formed similar opinions. During the 1940s, Diamond composed Concerto for Two Solo Pianos (1942), String Quartet No. 2 (1943), Symphony No. 3 (1945), String Quartet No. 3 (1946), Sonata for Piano (1947) and Chaconne for Violin and Piano (1948). He was, as Leonard Bernstein justifiably opined, a "vital branch in the stream of American music." However, his air of sophistication and accomplishment held little attraction for Kerouac. Seven years his senior, Diamond told Jack one December night that he was appalled by his behavior and reputation around the Village. Kerouac's drunken rowdiness was notorious at the San Remo Bar. Because of this, Diamond did not wish to endanger his reputation as an accomplished compser by being seen with him. Furthermore, Diamond said that he did not have a "mature sense of values," something that rang all too true to the oversensitive and paranoiac Kerouac. His reaction to Diamond's personal assessment was to call it "deeply untrue," rude, and insulting. Their relationship was further fractured when Diamond asked an appalled and resisting Kerouac to go to bed with him. It was, as Kerouac confided into his personal notebook, "an insult to my manhood after all."

Kerouac preferred to keep his nighttime hours warm with female companionship. One was a married woman named Pauline (Lucille in *On the Road*), who worked part-time as a model for artist Alan Wood-Thomas. Liana Thomas-Wade, the daughter of the artist, was six years old at the time (she is mentioned in Kerouac's journals as "Leanne," a little girl who, after taking a seat on his lap, made him feel "less of a monster"). Liana, remembering Pauline in 2007, said she reminded her of *La Dolce Vita*'s blond Swedish actress Anita Eckberg. To Kerouac, she resembled Carole Lombard. He naively imagined that, at some level, he and Pauline "understood each other." Alternatively, he felt pressured to do something "decisive" with her: "She is perhaps the great woman I sought, and I am perhaps the loving man she seeks." She was, in his eyes, an ideal candidate, despite her tenuous marital status, for a ranch wife.

There was also the startling Spanish/Peruvian beauty Adele Morales. At a dance sponsored by the New School, Kerouac first saw her from across the dance hall. She appeared to him as exotic and dark-looking. He approached her "before anyone else did." Though she thought him as "movie star handsome," she also intuited that he was "totally self-absorbed." In her account, after first meeting her, Kerouac spent more time jotting notes into his journal than speaking to her. He did admire her intelligence, enough so that he entrusted her with some manuscript pages of *The Town and the City*. She showed her mother the pages, and her less-than-flattering remark that he was "no Dickens," prompted Kerouac's curt reply, "Fuck you!" to Adele. If he was no writer, then her mother was no literary critic. His inability to handle any degree of criticism toward his writing usually resulted in a vicious string of invectives about the critic's lack of qualifications in judging his work. In his journal, he wrote: "I gave Adele parts of my novel to read. However the next night, she didn't turn out to be the warm sexy Spanish girl I figured her as—a kind of educated Bea Franco—it seems she is 'confused' and is being psychoanalyzed and so on." Furthermore, they "argued too much."

Nonetheless, Kerouac felt that his relations with women, as broad and frequent as they were, were lacking. Comparing himself to a "caveman," he realized that he initiated contact with women only to lay them. When a relationship evolved further, he usually bailed out. He was also confused about how women approached him. When Rae Everitt, a female friend of Ginsberg (later, Kerouac's first literary agent) became friendly with Kerouac, she backed off from his aggressive advances. Despondent, he compared himself to Melville's troubled protagonist in the short story "Bartleby the Scrivener." Bartleby's "depressive" and "catatonic" state as he retreated further and further into passive resistance, mirrored Kerouac's approach to responsibility. Bartleby's line of "preferring not to" in the past, present, and future, registers constantly in Kerouac's letters, journals, and published work.

In a similar analogy, Kerouac's mental state reflected Melville's Ishmael in *Moby Dick;* his desperation and alienation toward society urged him to move on, out and away from the city. Drawing a "blank" in his soul, Kerouac hung on desperately until it was time for him to leave, at last, to Cassady.

WAITING

Kerouac felt that Cassady was ignoring his letters. "Where are you man?" he urgently asked of Cassady in October 1948, "why is it you don't write to me when you know there's so many things that have got to be said." Kerouac was visiting Rocky Mount to be with his sister, who had just given birth to a boy, Paul Jr. It was a difficult delivery resulting in Caesarian birth. Gabrielle cared for her daughter and her granddaughter to ease the woes of the near-death state Nin suffered. Kerouac, sitting at a makeshift desk in a shack in the Blake's yard while the rain poured outside, spilled out his own distress at Cassady's neglect. "I'm really bugged because you stop writing sometimes. There's no need for that, just write steady like I do."

Cassady, as he usually did, responded to Kerouac because he was now in dire need of some kind of income. Though he had initially reinforced Kerouac's ranch ideas by gathering related pamphlets, his "All-American" friend never received them; Cassady had more important things to think about. He was now out of money and out of work after the Southern Pacific Railroad voted to cut down on their manpower. In desperation, he latched on to a friend, Al Hinkle (Ed Dunkel in *On the Road*), offering to drive him and his new wife Helen (Galatea Dunkel in *On the Road*) to New York for their honeymoon. Hinkle, also laid off from the Southern Pacific, had known Cassady since his youth. Cassady had been instrumental in bringing Al and Helen together in a hasty marriage ceremony to take advantage of the money he and Al thought Helen possessed.

Hinkle agreed to drive with Cassady, provided that he acquired a car. Hinkle came up with $100 and Cassady drained his family bank account, using it to put a down payment on a brand-new maroon 1949 Hudson. It was Neal's one and only payment toward the car. Excited, he placed a long-distance phone call on December 15 to the drugstore beneath Kerouac's Ozone Park apartment. Cassady informed Kerouac of his newest plans: "Yes, yes, it's Neal, you see . . . I'm calling you, see. I've got a '49 Hudson. . . ."

"And what are you going to do?"

"That's what I was going to say now. To save you the hitch-hiking trip out to the Coast, see, I will break in my new car, drive to New York, test it, see, and we will run back to Frisco as soon as possible, see, and then run back to Arizona to work on the railroads. I have jobs for us, see. Do you hear me, man?"

"I hear you, I hear you, see."

Cassady continued: "See, Al Hinkle is with me in the phone booth. Al is coming with me, he wants to go to New York. I will need him, see, to help me jack up the car in case I get a flat or in case I get stuck, see, a real helper and pal, see."

Kerouac, also an opportunist, began formulating plans of his own. If the unpredictable and unreliable Cassady *did* indeed arrive, he could drive himself and Gabrielle back to New York City, where she could await the arrival of her daughter's family to live with her in Ozone Park. Once in New York, he and Cassady could celebrate New Year's Eve together in Manhattan. Though Kerouac suspected Cassady had stolen the car, it was still an opportunity too appealing to pass up. It was also a way for the ever-frugal Kerouac to avoid spending too much money for his travels, thereby saving the stipend he was receiving again from the government. He expected Cassady's arrival in North Carolina on December 29. He terminated the phone call by offering to send Cassady fifty dollars to fund the trip (though he actually only sent ten). Even that was a mix-up. Cassady later phoned the store and told Gabrielle, who took the call because Kerouac was in New York City with Pauline, not to send the money in his name to his address, but under another name at a different address. It was too late.

It was an immeasurable relief for Kerouac and he was thrilled. Like a lovesick schoolgirl in her notebook, he singsonged in a letter to Ginsberg, "Neal is coming to New York, Neal is coming to New York for New Year's Eve."

Kerouac began planning; he asked Ginsberg to arrange a New Year's Eve party and invite "everybody." (As he was writing the letter, a child watched over his shoulder, amazed at the speed of his typing.) From there they could relocate to John Clellon Holmes's place and so on, until the night expired wherever they happened to drop. He would be with Pauline. For Cassady, Kerouac planned on asking Adele. Because Jack and his mother planned on spending Christmas in North Carolina with Nin, Cassady would have to pick him up there and drive them to the city. All in all it was everything he could hope for, an advantageous diversion to his current "life-problems." By chance and not design, he was about to take the trip, one magnified to mythical status in the second part of *On the Road*.

PART

2

CHAPTER FIVE

HUDSON HORNET

Neal Cassady had concealed his plans, impulsive, irrational, and selfish in execution *and* design, from Carolyn. Her life, up to now, mixed penury with bouts of absolute despondency. Baby bottles, soiled diapers, late nights and early mornings made for brutally unforgiving work made even more anxiety ridden by the prospect of poverty. Cassady was absent, sometimes for hours, more often for days on end.

Cassady revealed his intentions only by way of deception, informing Carolyn that he was in fact doing *favors,* that he was almost *obligated* to do favors—no matter that they hardly justified leaving her behind over the Christmas holidays. The car had not left a positive impression upon her, since they were living in a shoddy apartment sparsely furnished with orange crates. Nevertheless, Cassady persevered: "Now, now, Carolyn, look here, you don't understand. Al and Helen are getting married tomorrow, right? They have to have a honeymoon, but they have no car. Now, then, Jack wants to come out, but he hasn't the money to get here. So, see, ol' Cass to everybody's rescue." Besides, he reasoned, the car was important for Carolyn and the baby even if it wasn't actually going to be there when she needed it.

Not that Cassady totally lacked a conscience; he wrestled with the problem of maintaining his family in his absence. However, he sensed, accurately, the discord in his marriage only meant he would inflict further misery upon his wife. Hinkle's incessant badgering caused his conscience to support his departure. It was the last straw for Carolyn. Outraged, she told Cassady to leave if he was going to, and to not come back. Closing the door behind him, he did just that.

So the newlyweds, Al and Helen Hinkle, plus a paying traveling sailor they found lingering in a San Francisco travel bureau, stepped into the unheated Hudson with not a word between them, only accompanied by Cassady's incessant playing of the car radio and his rambling narratives. Soon after they left, Cassady lit up the first of numerous marijuana cigarettes. This casual air of illicit indulgence thoroughly shocked Helen Hinkle.

Twenty-two-year-old Helen Hinkle had met Neal Cassady only once—when he was best man at their wedding the day before. Understandably, she soon became afraid of his frenetic driving and his unpredictable, often selfish, demeanor. She came from a strict Seventh Day Adventist upbringing, and though she had left that church, she was, for her age, tremendously naive. Cassady's casual drug use, his drinking, smoking, and graphic sex talk coalesced into a frightful image of their honeymoon chauffeur as a sociopathic maniac. From that first day, she said little to Cassady and he, in turn, ignored her. To him, Helen Hinkle was good for money and little else (and even that she wanted to spend on hotel rooms instead of a mad marathon dash across America). Along the way, he picked up a mother with her epileptic child to whom Cassady displayed his congenial self. Helen remained less than pleased and opted to leave the men, to continue her travels alone by train.

They dropped Helen off in Tucson, Arizona, only clutching her husband's railroad pass. She was to take a train to New Orleans, where William Burroughs was waiting for Kerouac and company to arrive. They planned to pick her up in a week. (She in fact decided to stay in a hotel until Al arrived.) The sailor, heading home to Kansas, became discouraged when the car was not heading east, but south.

The Hudson then looped back north to pick up LuAnne Henderson in Denver, who was now engaged to a sailor currently out at sea. Without any immediate commitments at hand, she accepted Cassady's proposal to accompany him to wintry New York. In Denver, the disgusted sailor bailed. Unburdened of dead weight, the Hudson careened eastward toward North Carolina to pick up Kerouac.

ROCKY MOUNT

The rest of the trip to Rocky Mount was an odyssey of indigence and misery. Cassady had to open the car windows to prevent them from icing up. A man they picked up promised food, but all they found at his home was a pile of putrefying potatoes that LuAnne had to sort through for those worth frying. Before leaving, Cassady hustled the helpless man for what little change he had, and then struck him on the head.

At gas pump after gas pump, Cassady illegally rolled the numbers back before driving the "slow boat to China" (as it was later dubbed by Kerouac in *On the Road*) eastward. About one week after their departure, the car, with its tired and hungry occupants, arrived to a virtually unsuspecting family. It was Christmas Day. Inside the cozy house, with its burning hearth and the scent of baking bread and roasting meat, the Blakes and Kerouacs were enjoying a family Christmas (that was virtually nonexistent in the Cassady household). Gabrielle had arrived with Kerouac only a day earlier. She graciously assisted Nin with the turkey dinner and the care of her grandson. The Christmas tree, a-glimmer with festive lights and tinsel, stood above opened presents. Little Paul was excited to see his grandmother and uncle.

There was a knock on the door. Kerouac answered and saw Cassady, unkempt, dirty, and unshaven, shuffling his feet on the welcome mat. Peering out at the car, through the filthy windshield he saw two more figures sitting together in the front seat. Beckoned in by Kerouac, they entered feeling a little out of place.

The next day, Cassady made good on his promise to drive Gabrielle's belongings to Ozone Park with Kerouac. The foursome, including LuAnne and Al Hinkle, embarked on a trip that was, according to Kerouac in his journal, "memorable for the cold and dry misery." When they arrived in Ozone Park, Al and LuAnne stayed behind in Gabrielle's apartment. Cassady and Kerouac sped back to Rocky Mount to pick up Gabrielle and some of Nin's furniture to return to Brooklyn. On the way, Cassady earned himself a speeding ticket that Gabrielle paid from her little shiny purse after some harassment by the patrol car officer. Back in Ozone Park, they unloaded the furniture and settled themselves in for some after-hours partying before heading south to New Orleans and Algiers.

In approximately one week, Neal Cassady had driven 4,943 miles across the country (including Rocky Mount to New York twice).

NEW YEAR IN MANHATTAN

In New York, Allen Ginsberg was desperately trying to "normalize" his life. On December 1, 1949, he signed a lease for his own apartment at 1401 York Avenue, on the Upper East Side. The previous tenant, Walter Adams, fortunately left Allen some furniture. Allen's morale had been low, as he struggled with keeping a debilitating job. He was also concentrating upon his poetry and his reading, which became the saving graces of his existence. Confiding to Lionel Trilling that his job was "terrible," he dismissed it as nothing more than a "compromise with society." In sum, it was a lot of "B.S. to assume some phony responsibilities." Like Kerouac, he sensed the world's, and his own, chronic moroseness. His personal foundation was, he felt, crumbling. His levee against the world's poisoned waters was Baudelaire, e.e. cummings, St. Augustine, and Emily Dickinson (among a few others). The appearance of Cassady and Kerouac at this time, served both as a welcome distraction and further confusion for Ginsberg who, to some degree, remained enamored with Neal.

Kerouac and Cassady pursued a dizzying circuit of loft parties, all-night rap sessions and cheap jazz joints. They went to see the newly formed George Shearing Quintet. Jazz was beginning to transform once again. Shearing, in the same month Dean and Sal "dug him" (not at Birdland as noted in *On the Road*, for the club's actual opening did not occur until almost a year later, in December 1949), was about to release his first big hit, "September in the Rain" from the album of the same name released by MGM. Shearing's method of piano-playing, the "locked hand" technique he learned from Milt Buckner, called for playing parallel chords, which gave the feel of the band functioning as a single instrument. "September in the Rain"'s overnight success for Shearing introduced a whole new sound that changed the face of modern jazz. The excited pair "dug" him deeply.

Kerouac had his hands full with Cassady, who talked his ear off with characteristic ebullience. As Kerouac attempted to latch on to LuAnne physically, he was also trying to make it with Pauline wishing that he had enough money to support her and her child. The childless LuAnne won for the moment before Pauline drifted off. Her brief appearance as Lucille in *On the Road* remains her legacy. However, it was not the last he heard from her.

Kerouac excitedly shared his personal visions to Al Hinkle: wandering angels adrift in the city, legions of girls sitting alone in coffee shops or walking sexily along city sidewalks, and his "feelings for the road." There were also those moments, by turn tender and brutal, with Neal Cassady. Hinkle could testify to Cassady's temperament, a seething stew of unpredictability and reliability. Stoned on pot, Cassady could be congenial, and even display a semblance of Midwestern gentility. Other times he resorted to impulsive violence, as LuAnne found out more than once.

The new year gave Kerouac a feeling of heightened

expectations. He was pleased by knowing that his sister's family would soon arrive to live with Gabrielle, freeing him of the anxiety he felt whenever he left her alone for any length of time. Shame and guilt constantly welled up in him, and justifiably so. For the most part, his mother had supported him continuously since her husband's death up to then.

Within the first few weeks of the new year, the new canary yellow Ford convertible pulled up to the Ozone Park apartment. The Blakes moved into the apartment intending to make arrangements for more spacious living quarters. In the apartment, infant Paul slept in his grandfather's deathbed. Kerouac, already suffocated by his own mortality, craved life, even more life than he could ever live. "Life," he wrote, was like a "sea" enveloping his "thirsty island's mouth."

The automobile trip was, at this point, a certainty though he still vaguely planned on returning to sea in a few weeks with Cassady and Ginsberg. He also kept on the back burner plans to accompany Ed White to Paris. By his own admission, Kerouac was also responsible for earning some income to help pay for his and his mother's rent, a fact made even more pressing when Paul Blake Sr. announced that he might possibly buy an eight-room New Jersey farmhouse for the family.

• • •

For now, Doctor Sax's reddened dusk settling upon the shrouded West reigned over Kerouac's creative imagination. Shrugging off a slew of papers he was supposed to write for the classes he hardly attended anymore, he and his brother-in-law went to see *Red River*, a Howard Hawks film starring John Wayne and Montgomery Clift. Infusing and enhancing Kerouac's colorful notions of the West, it told the story of a pair of father-and-son cattle ranchers traveling west to California facing an uncertain future. It was just the right fuel to stoke *On the Road*'s full realization. He thought it a "great picture."

In matters of destiny, he had reason to believe that he, Cassady, and Ginsberg were being led by God on their own separate paths of fate. Kerouac's fate was to "make up for my crime by learning all and laboring great books." Cassady's was to answer his burning question: why he had to deceive people to get through life. Allen was being led from the "circle-swirls" of life, a consequence of his banishment from the same. Lastly, Kerouac wrote, Gabrielle was being led heavenward to reside with the "exploited saints" of the physical world. His conclusion, "There are no problems, see?" inevitably found its way into the mouth of Dean Moriarty in *On the Road* (as well as the next statement, "*I* know God"—altered to "*We* know God").

Carolyn Cassady received a letter from her husband, postmarked January 11. In it, he promised her regular installments of cash from working two jobs in New York, neither of which he had yet to procure. He confessed to pangs of guilt: "My heart is heavy. As I reread your letters, I feel heavy depression." According to Cassady, the pain he felt inside, even through his marijuana-induced euphoria, was "indescribable." He assured his wife that even though he did not have a job as of yet, he would find one soon. Once he did, he would send her his paycheck, less ten dollars for his living expenses. Cassady made another empty promise, to sell the Hudson, knowing full well that he had planned on returning to San Francisco with it (without ever actually paying for it). Enclosed with the letter was eighteen dollars, courtesy of Kerouac's GI benefits. "So I'll take care of car & you too. I wound all the people I love—why?" This last may have been the only part of the letter that was true.

It was only through the assistance of a railroading acquaintance of Cassady's that Carolyn endured these times at all. After he left, a man named Ardo came to her door. His zeal to please Cassady induced in Carolyn a plethora of "mixed emotions" despite her virtual dependency upon him. His presence meant her husband's absence, which in turn only enhanced her confusion and loneliness. However, Ardo's presence also guaranteed a much-needed supply of food, diapers, and other necessities she couldn't afford at the moment.

Still, she had the fortitude to tell him that he was a fool for listening to Cassady at all, that her husband conned people, and that he was a thief and liar. Ardo, who looked up to Cassady, defended his friend's character. Carolyn asked: "How can you believe a man who deserts his wife and baby?" Her disgust for Cassady was only made stronger one day when Ardo came to the house brandishing a postcard from his hero. She took it from him to read it and noticed the Denver postmark; Neal was picking up or at least visiting LuAnne Henderson.

But LuAnne had her share of troubles, too. Kerouac notes that Cassady "beat up Louanne [*sic*]." The shiny ideal of Cassady as a "western hero" began evaporating when he and Lucien watched, shocked, as Cassady struck LuAnne. Kerouac, as enamored as he was of her, did not come to her defense. Instead, he remained a silent spectator. Furthermore, Cassady was stealing money from Kerouac's friends. At the Clique Club (where Miles Davis that year further experimented with the nonet, thus ushering in the "Birth of the Cool"), Cassady pinched two dollars from Lucien's wallet. Kerouac dismissed these more unattractive traits, feeling mildly intrigued by Cassady's "savagery."

"I BURN"

"That whore," Kerouac spat into his journal. Pauline was distracting him from the feverish debaucheries he was enjoying with Cassady. He was still unhappy at how their relationship had ended, even though he was the cause of its dissolution. In a letter, she attacked Kerouac's work ethic, his writing, and what she deemed his skewed spirituality. Angrily, she informed Kerouac that he would end up in hell on the business end of Satan's pitchfork:

> My husband isn't a bastard like the likes of you. You couldn't even polish his shoes. The pity of it all is this, that I can't get you to go out and work. I'd make you work so down hard the sweat would fall from your brow like the rain you keep talking about. That's the only thing that will save you, Work, Manual Labor [. . .] I suggest that you try writing about *real people* like us and not jerks like Doctor Sax and his rainy nights. Don't ever call yourself a religious writer again, you don't know your ass from a hole in the ground about religion. You brought me down to your level, but that won't be for long.

An angry vengeful husband was all Kerouac needed to prompt his instant departure in Neal's car.

There was Helen Hinkle, also angry, awaiting news from her husband. Her host, a perturbed William Burroughs, posted letters north at a rapidly accelerating rate. To Ginsberg on January 10, he wrote, "What kind of a character is this Hinckle [*sic*] to leave his wife here without funds, then not even bother to let her know what his intentions are?" Six days later, he sent another letter.

> I would like to know what gives with the Hinckle-Kerouac-Cassady expedition. Does this Hinckle character expect to billet his wife on me indefinitely? His performance is an all time record for sheer gall and irresponsibility. I have never so much as laid eyes on Hinckle. Behavior like his would stretch a close friendship.

How Al Hinkle treated Helen was of no concern to Burroughs, but his doing so at the expense of Burroughs's money and time was driving the latter to distraction. After all, Burroughs's funds were hard won. He was making an earnest attempt to produce his own positive cash flow. His crop of peas, his first true agricultural venture, had frozen five days before harvest, costing him a potential windfall of $5,000. He was more fortunate with the lettuce crop, having sold eight acres worth at $250. More daring was his illicit prospect of "putting out feelers in the junk market." He wanted to sell dope for the fast cash flow from the "swarm of junkies" in New Orleans. In desperation, he noted that the New Orleans junkies "outbid each other" for the privilege of doing business with one, a fact making it impossible to kick heroin; one never had to go looking for business, "it comes looking for you."

A MISTY SAGA OF THE NIGHT

The car sped beneath the Hudson River, coming out of the tunnel, reemerging into the bleak misty night. The radio was playing bebop and, jubilantly, Kerouac drummed the erratic rhythms of bebop on the Hudson dashboard. Their differences settled, Cassady sat next to LuAnne with Kerouac at her right. In the backseat, Al Hinkle was sitting with a woman he met named Rhoda. What they did in the dark only enlivened the imagination of Kerouac, who wrote into his journal that they were "making love." The trio in the front seat rhapsodized the words that were put into the mouth of Carlo Marx in *On the Road*: "Whither goest thou America in thy shiny car at night?" Jubilant with glee at finally leaving the city, despite his feeling of being "haunted," Kerouac was beside himself with joy. In the not-too-distant future, he would see Bill Burroughs, for the first time in months, with his main inspiration, Neal Cassady (an attraction that many others had yet to sort out). Kerouac anticipated this meeting of two minds, almost positive that Cassady's swift thinking and con-man rap would appeal to Burroughs's street sensibilities.

The car raced into the state of Maryland and, somewhere outside of Baltimore, Cassady veered from Route One onto a winding tar road. They lost themselves in a tangle of dark forest. "Doesn't look like Route One," wrote Kerouac in *On the Road,* preserving the casual aside. Retracing their route, the car was back on the main highway and speeding south at a constant and reassuring pace. By dawn, the sun was rising east of the nation's capital. On the streets of Washington, D.C., a massive array of "war machines" were lined up awaiting the presidential inauguration parade for Harry S. Truman. They stopped in a coffee shop, Hinkle stole a coffee cake for the starving travelers. Rhoda, wisely, boarded a bus and returned to New York.

Al Hinkle took the wheel through Virginia, but before he even cleared the city line of Richmond, he was pulled over by a patrol car. Cassady handed his stash of marijuana to a compliant LuAnne, demanding that she stuff it down her pants. After the police officer asked who she was (he suspected that she hadn't yet turned eighteen), she blurted out that she was Cassady's wife. Cassady responded that she was in fact his ex-wife and that they were on their way to see his current wife. Hidden marijuana stash withstanding, the point of the inquisition was the Mann Act, which outlawed the transporting of females for "immoral purposes." (Even Gabrielle had been subjected to this when she was riding with Cassady and Kerouac back to Brooklyn a few weeks before.) The first person to be prosecuted under the Mann Act was heavyweight boxer Jack Johnson. He got caught driving across state lines with a prostitute who he had convinced to leave her brothel. In 1944, Charles Chaplin was also arrested with actress Joan Barry. Others over the years included architect Frank Lloyd Wright, rocker Chuck Berry, and murderer Charles Manson. This law would plague Cassady and Kerouac more than once as they trekked through

America. The arrest enraged Cassady, especially after they had to pay a fine of fifteen dollars for vagrancy charges. Cassady vowed to return to the county and kill the arresting officer for the fine came at a great material sacrifice: Hinkle's railroad watch, LuAnne's new diamond engagement ring, and cash from Kerouac's wallet.

Cassady's mood altered when they picked up the first of a slew of hitchhikers. Though most vowed to contribute money, most did not follow through. Oftentimes, after entering through the front door, they disappeared out the back. Though his driving skills were minimal at best, Kerouac took the wheel for limited stretches, to let the others sleep. As he drove, he brooded about his work, pondering all that sped by in the sleepy hours of South Carolina.

As the air began to warm and the trees turned green, before long the car reached Mobile, Alabama. The others woke up and agreed to spend the last of their money on food. For gas, Cassady was happy to steal what they needed, much to Kerouac's apprehension (though he regarded the act as a "divine theft"). Roughly 150 miles later, they were finally in the state of Louisiana.

NEW ORLEANS WITH OLD BULL LEE

When Helen Hinkle reached New Orleans, she still had enough money to rent a room for a few days before the Sugar Bowl began to make it impossible to rent a room anywhere.

Calling Burroughs, she agreed to meet him at a Chinese restaurant. Her first impression of him was though he was only thirty-five years old, he had the demeanor of someone of at least ninety-five. After she shared her predicament, Burroughs invited her to stay at his place until her husband arrived. Burroughs was generous even to the extent that he was ready to convert a vacant chicken shed into living quarters for Helen and Al.

From the start, Helen made herself less of a burden by leaving the house in the morning and returning at nightfall. What she did observe for the time being was the oddness of the family. Whereas Neal was just plain creepy to her, the Burroughses exuded an odd gentility. By night, when the moon loomed over the yard, Joan endlessly swept anoles from an ugly bare tree. As the others slept, she constantly mopped the floor or scrubbed the walls. Helen didn't know of Joan's addiction to Benzedrine. Joan, however, took advantage of Helen's visits into town to purchase her Benzedrine inhalers. Though Helen was offered a dozen of them (the druggist assumed she wasn't the abusing type), she settled for only one. Joan lamented the lost opportunity. The children defecated into Revere Ware pots that were then washed and used for cooking. The food they ate, however, seemed healthy and, by Helen's account, the meals were well balanced, at least enough so that Helen could forget her disgust at what the pans had been used for before.

She also noted that Burroughs was fond of his weaponry,

often taking to firing at Benzedrine capsules. He was building a table that would last for a "thousand years" despite the worm-eaten condition of the wood. Thirteen cats were bathed before being tied together with string. Odd, true, but not as unpleasant or intimidating as Neal Cassady. Helen's assessment of Cassady grew more negative the longer she waited for Al—his prolonged absence had to have *something* to do with Neal. She confided to Burroughs that Cassady smoked pot and that he was the "devil incarnate." She had no clue that Burroughs was a drug addict himself. It was Helen's opinion that he used marijuana solely to work up an appetite to eat. "Heroin," he told her, was the "true evil."

Eventually the Hudson crossed the dark Mississippi aboard the Algiers ferry. Kerouac watched the rolling mist drift over the brownish water. On deck, they could see the light of the ferry's boiler shining like a beacon. He and LuAnne peered over the boat watching the stern knife through the muddy waters with a hiss. The following day Kerouac read about a girl's suicide from that very boat, and he pondered at length in his journal what she had to be thinking to take her life: "What horror was there in mossy New Orleans, what real final sadness did she see?"

Once crossing, they drove through Algiers's streets, passing the levee, high, digging the southern scenes. They smelled gumbo in the air, the smell of "piss," the rain squalls curtaining the Gulf, and the raw Mississippi itself rolling through America before discharging the country into the great Gulf of Mexico. The radio played the *Chicken Jazz n' Gumbo Show* as people sat on porches watching passersby. The muddied Hudson with its wearied occupants crept along unpaved roads. Cassady had put the new car through hell in less than two months. Burroughs felt Cassady could never resell it for half of what it was worth when he heard Neal would sell it.

The Hudson coupe, its bearings hoisy and shot, creaked into the dirt drive. Kerouac hesitantly opened the back door into the kitchen. It was the first time Helen had ever seen Kerouac. Behind him was Neal with LuAnne, whom he introduced as his "wife" despite the fact that he had already introduced Carolyn as the same only weeks earlier. Helen yanked Al into a bedroom. LuAnne followed, sitting down on a bench, and asked to watch if they were going to "screw."

Kerouac tried to fill the awkward hour by offering to make *crêpes suzette* from his own recipe. Burroughs had been fond of Kerouac ever since New York. Unlike Cassady, who made Burroughs feel he had to constantly be on guard from an impending con-job, Jack was endearing and genuine. During this visit, Burroughs spent more time with him than anybody else. Kerouac put a positive spin on the visit. The front porch was trellised, the yard blown by fresh breezes, and the sky seemed to be always blue, puffy clouds drifting over the Mississippi Valley.

Outside, Burroughs strapped a holster on Kerouac and played quick-draw with cap guns. Leaning like a wizard from his favorite chair, Burroughs told stories, mostly aiming his morphine-drawled monologue at Kerouac. The stories usually ranged from stories about New York to inquiries about and suggestions for Kerouac's writing. All this attention to Kerouac caused unease for Cassady. Not long after their arrival, Cassady sensed no funds were forthcoming and made plain his plans to leave as soon as possible. "He couldn't leave quick enough," Burroughs wrote to Allen Ginsberg after they had left. Al and Helen chose to stay behind. Al had a lead on a job in New Orleans and, with this stroke of fortune, could at least plan on staying for a few months longer. This time, after learning the hard way, they withheld from Cassady thirty dollars wired to them by a family member.

Burroughs was concerned for Kerouac and advised him against leaving with Cassady. He explained to Ginsberg: "I can not forego a few comments on the respective and comparative behavior of the several individuals composing this tour, a voyage which for sheer compulsive pointlessness compares favorably with the mass migrations of the Mayans. To cross the continent for the purpose of transporting Jack to Frisco where he intends to remain for 3 days before starting back to N.Y. . . . Obviously, the "purpose" of the trip is carefully selected to symbolize the basic fact of purposelessness" (WB to AG, January 30, 1949). Cassady, the "very soul of this voyage into pure, abstract, meaningless motion," was to the intuitive Burroughs (who certainly knew a con artist when he saw one), "the Mover." Cassady was compulsively and absurdly dedicated to moving *somewhere, anywhere,* just as long as he was *going;* he was willing to sacrifice anything: wife, child, friendship, "even his very car itself to the necessity of moving from one place to another," Burroughs wrote. "Neal *must* move."

ON THE ROAD AGAIN

And move he did. Kerouac had his mother wire him twenty-five dollars for gas and oil, which was immediately seized by Cassady. Whether Kerouac knew it or not (and most extant evidence points to the fact that he did), he was enabling Cassady by greasing the cogs of his selfishness and compulsion to move. He could have just as easily used the money to return home on a bus (as Burroughs advised).

Burroughs also dispensed some sound advice to Ginsberg. Herbert Huncke was about to be released from Riker's Island prison and, for the moment, had no place to go to. Ginsberg was pondering the idea of letting Huncke bunk up in his apartment. Burroughs wrote to Ginsberg that the "more obligation Huncke's under to anyone [. . .], the more certain he is to steal from or otherwise take advantage of his benefactor" (WB to AG, January 30, 1949). Ginsberg's rejection of this advice would cause dire circumstances in the months to come. The Hudson left at dusk with Neal Cassady again at the wheel, Jack Kerouac on the passenger side, and "honeycunt," as Cassady derogatorily referred to LuAnne, sitting docile in between. They waved good-bye to everyone and headed back to the ferry before disembarking at Canal Street.

They drove northeast through the bayous of Louisiana, to Baton Rouge, escorted at first only by night's violet hour. The dusk was muggy and dense, exuding the pungent smell of swamp. Lengthy fronds of willow trees hung like the hair of hippie giants. For the occasion, Kerouac put on his Shadow voice and narrated the events of the death of David Kammerer at the hands of Lucien Carr. The darkness, the spookiness of Kerouac's baritone, and Cassady's maniacal giggling put LuAnne in "shivers." After a while, Cassady drove with a grimace and LuAnne slept. As the miles piled up behind them, Cassady grew increasingly remote, as if the thrill of being with the other two was already beginning to wear.

Rain spat, scattered on the windshield. Seeing the Mississippi, the "Water of Life, the Water of Night," only brought Kerouac thoughts of "rain and rivers." The magic and mystery of a river, according to him, was that it bundled with a unifying thread all of mankind. At Baton Rouge they crossed the bridge into Port Allen, which brought to mind the river of his childhood, the Merrimack, sweeping its seething springtime torrent down the cascades of New Hampshire before turning northeast at Lowell, wending its way toward the Atlantic Ocean. He had seen the Merrimack's springtime thaw flood his beloved city, watched people already stung by the wasp of the Great Depression vacating destitute homes and businesses ruined for good (like his father's). Still, he imagined it as a supernatural force giving fuel to his Doctor Sax fantasy-myth.

Through the plains of Louisiana Cassady drove, into DeQuincy and Starks before stopping for gas in Opelousas. Kerouac bought some bread and cheese, measuring out his spending frugally. Mystery programs on the radio passed time as the delta crept thicker and denser until at one point Cassady stopped the car and turned off the headlights, immersing them in the "mireful, drooping dark." When he turned on the lights again, a thick jungle of creeping vines engulfed the car amid the clamor of screaming insects.

The car's endurance was further tested in the vast expanse of the Texan Panhandle. They crossed the state line at Beaumont, Texas. Oil fields replaced the bayou; Kerouac utilized the scenery as the backdrop for some of the early versions of *On the Road.* Not far was Ruston, Texas, the home of Big Slim, the vagrant who was searching for *something.* Cassady, knowing Texas's vastness, informed them that they could be driving all day long and still be in Texas the following night. Sometimes LuAnne took the wheel, other times it was Kerouac. During his shift, rain poured; headlights made lights dance on the spattered windshield. Once, the oncoming lights seemed to be coming straight at them. He swerved into a morass of mud in a ditch. The occupants of the other car were drunk and Kerouac, stunned, helped push the Hudson out of the mud. LuAnne was at the wheel, he and Cassady on their knees in torrents of rain, until the car finally heaved itself out after a half hour. Cold and exhausted, they slept as she drove. When Jack awoke, the car was in snowy Fredericksburg, Texas. Neal did not awake.

The next day was no different. Again they feasted on bread and cheese. Through the Pecos Valley, they got high; All three stripped nude, letting the sun bake their famished bodies. At one point they cavorted in the golden Texas light until a car approached. Kerouac and LuAnne hid and watched from inside the car as a pair of senior citizens gaped at Cassady posing like a statue high up on the side of the road.

In El Paso, Cassady looked for ways to find money. The travel bureau had no takers going west. A reform-school buddy was useless to them, even suggesting mugging somebody for cash. Cassady decided to chance it to Tucson where their pal Alan Harrington [Hal Hingham in *On the Road*] could feed them a hot meal and lend the cash needed to continue on to San Francisco. Through the days, Kerouac absorbed details of the western lands later incorporated into a 1950 version of *On the Road.* However, for the moment, he could not do the same for Cassady. "When someone we dote upon turns to us from his immortal solitary posture and seeks to speak to us, to communicate, to cadge, cavil, enjoin, persuade, anoint, or impress, with appropriate expressions and exertions, we see, instead of the loving image, a kind of new horrible revelation of reality, so suddenly existent." It was an unsettling paradox. Kerouac sensed LuAnne's genuine love for Cassady, and his own uncontained glee, yet knowing that the "false, flirtatious smile" Cassady flashed back to those watching him was sometimes hollow and insincere.

The final week of January brought the car's arrival to San Francisco. Tired, hungry with one battered suitcase and scarcely a penny between them, Cassady left Jack and LuAnne on the sidewalk. Burroughs was right; they had been conned out of their cash and deserted by him just as suddenly as he had appeared in their lives. LuAnne had sensed since New York that Cassady was pushing her and Kerouac together. Now they were, for better or for worse.

'FRISCO

Cassady's destination was Carolyn's new address, where he shuffled his feet, acting almost as if nothing had happened. His rap was as smooth as a jaded salesman who no longer found the sell a challenge. Though Carolyn wanted to remain cold toward him, she longed for his companionship and security. Cassady, when he put his will and being into it, possessed a tremendous work ethic.

"Now then . . . darling."

Carolyn fended off Cassady's advances knowing that the same hand that reached for her had also groped LuAnne. He left, making clear the fact that he was now essentially penniless and homeless. The next morning he called and pleaded to be allowed to return and begin anew their lives together. Before long he got his way. He promised to return the next day with Kerouac.

Kerouac had spent the last night with LuAnne in a hotel room on O'Farrell Street. They lay on a bed clothed as he told her of the Great World Snake, the mythical serpent of Dr. Sax's apocalypse. She listened absently. Now that they were finally alone, the spark was no longer there. Later, she went across a street. He saw her talk to an old, balding man and leave in a car with another woman. Standing in the shadows across the street, Kerouac tried signalling her by flicking a lit cigarette into the gutter.

Destitute, he trudged along Market Street wondering if Cassady was with Carolyn. He was lost, alienated, and alone. "I stopped dead in my tracks and shivered and tingled all over from top to toe; it was one of the most tremendous sensations of my life. For one full second I had no consciousness whatever of where I was, or even that I was anywhere on any sidewalk of the world; I was completely alone." He stood enraptured for ten seconds, soaking in the uniqueness of the moment, equating it with "beatitude." It was the epiphany of the whole trip, and he would use it as a seminal moment of self-realization in *On the Road.*

DEAN, CAMILLE, AND SAL

It was an awkward triangle, for the moment. Cassady tried his best to place himself back into Carolyn's good graces. Kerouac, all too aware of Neal's extracurricular excursions with LuAnne, did the same. They goofed around, trying to raise a smile in Carolyn. For work, Cassady arrived one day with a box of pots and pans he was planning to sell door to door. Carolyn stayed mum watching him go through his motions. Days later, she gathered the pans together placing them in a box for his supervisor to pick them up.

Once Cassady was securely established with Carolyn, he made plans to "dig jazz" with Kerouac. By the close of the week, the phone rang in the one-room apartment. Carolyn answered to hear the chirping young voice of LuAnne asking for her husband. Carolyn's disgust resurfaced once again.

Nothing had changed, nor would it ever. Confronting him, her anger flashed like the dark Mississippi clouds Kerouac had watched streaking the sun. To defend him, Kerouac explained that *he* had in fact a date with LuAnne, and that she stood him up. He proceeded to discredit her character as well. Though their insults of LuAnne pleased Carolyn, they were as false as Cassady's lame apologies.

Kerouac's last night with Cassady, for now, was spent in Richmond at a "wild jazz and whore joint," smoking tea and cavorting with girls who looked like Billie Holiday. Earlier that day, Kerouac called his mother, who wired him twenty-five dollars. Once he received it, he bought a loaf of bread, some cold cuts, and a bus ticket. He made some sandwiches for the trip and put them in his suitcase. Cassady and LuAnne accompanied him to the Third Street bus station. Frugal Kerouac refused to give any of his sandwiches to Cassady.

SAL RETURNS HOME

The bus first went to Portland, Oregon, seven hundred miles north of San Francisco. In a chili restaurant where the bus stopped to refuel, Kerouac first wrote of the Northern California cities he had passed through: little boys playing, American towns shining with the morning's wet glimmer, mountain lakes, thin air, an empty basketball court, creaking timbers, scenic snow peaks, visions of "Shaman Fools" traipsing behind him, hauntingly conjured in the vision of the Shrouded Stranger in *On the Road*. Kerouac amused himself by talking to two rumpled panhandlers who exited the bus at The Dalles. The greater the distance from San Francisco, the more his anger softened toward Cassady and LuAnne.

Reveries incited sleep through the Columbia River Valley, and a blizzard blanketed Washington State. In Butte, Montana, he recorded a one-page slice of prose titled "Butte Montana." He also wrote in a postcard to Allen Ginsberg that he was at the "sources of the rainy night, where the Missouri River starts—and the Powder Snake Yellowstone and the Big Horn & others—to roll in the tidal midland night down to Algiers bearing Montana logs past the house where Old Bill sits." This chain of mystical thought, "rain and rivers," something *lost,* was also later realized in the Shrouded Stranger's steps through the shadowy highway seeking redemption. Excitedly, he footed the postcard all in capital letters: ". . . MORE, MORE, MUCH MUCH MORE. . . . (I GOT IT)" (JK to AG, February 7, 1949).

Day after day, the landscape crept by. Mountains, valleys, broken plains, and rivers wending through the nation, all of them uniquely American. He considered all of it useful for *On the Road*. He noted that one book in a Montana drugstore window, titled *Yellowstone Red,* was *their* epic, their own *Iliad.* Men eating with their women wearing buckskin jackets and cowboy hats; children scattered around them, the next generation unique to their own, bestowing their magical western heritage. Sometimes, the magic was more than he could bear.

The "discovery of the astonishing spirit of the modern West," happened in North Dakota. In the bitter cold of the Dakota Badland, the snowdrifts glowed with a ghostly persistence. Before long, the snow caused traffic on the highway. Kerouac watched men in sheepskin jackets shovel in twenty-five-degrees-below Fahrenheit weather. The bus slid along the perilous roadway, sometimes gaining ground, sometimes losing it. Despite the adversities, a blissful Kerouac, who didn't have to be involved with the very real troubles brewing outside of his passenger window, decided that he wished he could have been born and raised–and die–in Dickinson, North Dakota.

The bus's engine caught fire in Bismarck, North Dakota, the very center of the state. The passengers waited in a diner while the vehicle was repaired. The journey resumed and Kerouac fell asleep, waking up, refreshed, in Fargo, North Dakota, where the temperature had plunged to a brutal thirty degrees below zero.

The rest of the trip was uneventful. Minnesota was nothing more to Kerouac than endless tracts of flat frozen fields punctuated by abrupt church steeples. The dreary gray-brown east was still ensnared in the the grip of winter. "How dull it was to be in the East again . . . no more raw hopes," Kerouac extolled in his journal.

In Toledo, Kerouac harbored hopes of seeing his ex-wife once again. He hitchhiked three rides into Detroit, but Edie wasn't home, according to her mother. With his last eighty-five cents in his pocket, he roamed the quiet streets "more beat than ever." Inside, he raged. Edie's family had spoken to him on the phone as if he were a "bum," refusing to lend him three dollars to eat. Exhausted and starving, he went into the library and read up on the Oregon Trail. His concern wasn't eating or even sleeping, but how the world viewed him, how the Parkers were treating him. What did he do to Edie that was so bad it made them think less of him? Despite his disenchantment, his anger toward Neal was gone. Life was too short to hold grudges, as the Parkers were holding against him: "We part, we wander, we *never* return. I die here" (WW, 314).

At the Detroit bus depot, Kerouac "fumed with rage" on the men's room floor. He was approached by a preacher extolling the virtues of the Lord. He spent his last dime on Skid Row for a "cheap meal." Remembering in *On the Road,* Kerouac wrote: "My whole wretched life swam before my weary eyes, and I realized no matter what you do it's bound to be a waste of time in the end so you might as well go mad. All I wanted was to drown my soul in my wife's soul and reach her through the tangle of shrouds which is flesh in bed. At the end of the American road is a man and woman making love in a hotel room."

In Pennsylvania, Kerouac stole apples from a country store. He felt lonely, despondent, drained. It was February 1949. Kerouac was home now after an eight-thousand-mile trip (his estimate), in time to resume classes at New School and begin life anew. He was charged from his most recent journey across America. In the quiet, dark kitchen, he cooked himself a dish of bacon and eggs. The next day, he registered for classes. For now, *On the Road* would wait until he could formulate a new approach for it. He resumed writing *Doctor Sax,* a work he sensed was increasingly imbued with the darkness that possessed him through the bottomless pockets of America.

CHAPTER SIX

On the Road Developments

The end of March brought Kerouac good fortune. *The Town and the City* had been accepted for publication by Harcourt, Brace. He penciled prayers of thanks to God in his journal. His labors were now justified, and his plans of being a novelist were secure. He was also now one thousand dollars richer.

On April 27, 1949, in the throes of completing *The Town and the City,* Kerouac began to handwrite one of the earliest versions of *On the Road,* less than three months after his first cross-country trip with Neal Cassady in January. Along with it, he devised an "itinerary" from which he based his planned novel. To his friend Alan Harrington, he wrote, "I start to work in earnest on my 2nd novel this week. 'On the Road.' I think."

Ginsberg, during his Texas hiatus with Cassady, had jotted into his journal that he was attempting to interest Cassady into writing an "American picaresque" along the same lines as Kerouac's novel. Ginsberg envisioned it to be full of "nature and events, a chain of deeds and darings and sufferings and mad kicks and slow developments and purgation and final purity and intellectual beauty and physical vigor at the end." To help Cassady along, Ginsberg created a reading list comprising in part of Stendhal, Céline, *Don Quixote,* Cellini, Hart Crane, Baudelaire, Rimbaud, and Rilke. Ginsberg sensed that Cassady's writing would have to be a purely American work. This conclusion was drawn by Ginsberg's sense that his lost lover was "wide, aware, awake, experienced" and that he was blessed with a "true individuality." For the novel to be written, it had to be "straightly told," and "dramatic." By novel's end, it would "burst with joy and consummation." Whether or not Ginsberg apprised Kerouac of his suggestion to Cassady, it seems that applying the genre of American picaresque to Neal Cassady, or of a character like him in the novel's early stages, were the makings of a good book.

In this new work, there was to be a handful of characters: Red Moultrie; Vern; Vern's father, Old Vern ("the lost father he never found"); and Smitty. Red realizes after being sprung from three years in jail that "*every moment counts.*" The world the rest have taken for granted is seized upon like a starving hawk. Red is in a "trance" lasting for the few weeks it takes to complete his pilgrimage to the golden West. Kerouac inserted into the draft references to a lost inheritance, lost relations, and spirituality elusive to reach, evasive to find.

Kerouac's family continued to trouble him with their legitimate concerns over rising debts. The fact that he was about to receive an advance and that his hard work was about to be justified by a published book did little to increase his family's faith in him. However, he was not about to let them deter him. He was in the process of refashioning his ideas and realigning his aesthetic. The previous eight months had hatched a batch of poetry and a work-in-progress based upon the merging of his boyhood in Lowell, Massachusetts, and the radio serial, *The Shadow.* Elements of the novel *Doctor Sax* later seeped into *On the Road,* but for now they resided in separate spheres of Kerouac's creative psyche. With his recent experience, he felt his prose was now "different," certainly much more sophisticated in its voice and confidence than the novel to be published. To maintain this consistency, Kerouac knew to shun his family's petty squabbles, the world's concern at large and his own uncertainties. He had to "keep the flow" in a narrative that was now "richer in texture." More important, he would "write as far opposite from contemporary prose as possible" (Windblown World, 182).

On the Road would be populated with those outcasts addressed by Whitman in "Song of the Open Road." America was still seething with racial prejudice and the clash of the social classes. Those who never found stable ground after being cut loose from the American mainstream during the years of the Great Depression had now fallen into oblivion. For the time being, they remained wandering vagrants, railroad "bums," highway hoboes relentlessly searching America for a lucky break. They were the people that Spengler addressed in *The Decline of the West*. Kerouac incorporated Spengler's ideas into his world-reality. Closeted homosexuals, stifled minorities, shunned drug addicts, each sapped of hope or support from the society that helped put them there. These were the *fellah-people* Spengler addressed. He wrote:

> All Civilizations enter upon a stage, which lasts for centuries, of appalling depopulation. The whole pyramid of cultural man vanishes. It crumbles from the summit, first the world-cities, then the provincial forms, and finally the land itself, whose best blood has incontinently poured into the towns, merely to bolster them up awhile. At the last, only the primitive blood remains, alive, but robbed of its strongest and most promising elements. This residue is the *Fellah type*." (Spengler, 105)

This description applied loosely but accurately to most of Kerouac's characters in his mature fiction and poetry. The poet LeRoi Jones observed: "[Hubert] Selby's hoodlums, Burroughs's addicts, Kerouac's mobile young voyeurs, my own Negroes, are literally not included in the mainstream of American life." Society's dropouts and outcasts, however, predominated in Kerouac's writing. Neal Cassady, the ultimate American tragi-con of dropouts, provided him with a convenient vehicle in *On the Road.*

The novel's progression, from loose, random ideas, spreads out over the course of several lengthy notebooks from 1947 to 1957. That decade documents Kerouac's remarkable transformation: a stoic struggle to refine his writing and ideas in abject poverty; a growing alienation from the stifling post–World War II social conformity; a determination to follow the erratic footsteps of his creative spirit; and the pursuit of an elusive goal to forge a "life-changing" art form.

The ideas for *On the Road* were still centered on characters he had developed previously. However, he started bridging them to some of the New York characters in *The Town and the City* with the idea that the key ingredient to writing was in creating contrast. Therefore, a believable character must possess both the divine and the flawed. He decided to eliminate the Ray Smith character from the storyline and, instead, use him as narrator. The "hero" of the story would be much like himself, in his late twenties and having "lived a lot." He was a jailbird who realizes once he is behind bars that he needs to search out an "incorruptible, undefined" inheritance "that not fadeth away." He had a lost father somewhere out West and, upon his release from jail, planned to search for him. Accompanying him was an "almost idiotic boy" Kerouac compared to Ahab's Pip, possessed of a "nature too sweet, too saintly for this world."

Kerouac also started working the concept of being *beat* into the novel. The character must not only be indigent, but homeless as well. He lacks the consolation and sorrow of a family, has nobody on this living earth to turn to, and therefore survives solely by his skills and wits; a "kind of mystic signification" exuding an "exterior air of pilgrimage." For the first time Kerouac linked the character to a synthesis of Neal Cassady and Al Hinkle. Before Moultrie's incarceration, he was married to a woman resembling Bea Franco in California, one of the first hints that Kerouac planned on utilizing their idyllic romance in *On the Road*. The hero was motherless at birth; his earliest memory is of a crisp blue morning and a brown Colorado mountainside. His wife, despondent, gives up on him during his three years in prison.

On the Road was also to be a grand study of the geographical tapestry of American valleys, mountains, rivers, towns, and cities. That was the "rockbound spine of it," as Lowell and New York City were the backbone for *The Town and the City*. Three unifying concepts would also tie the work together: the four seasons of America, individual places in America, and the anguished entitlement for an inheritance. Springtime was to be emphasized in New York City, along with the Mississippi River, the American South in general, and New Orleans in particular. Summer was the ideal for depicting the plains and mountains of the Midwest, Nebraska, Iowa, and the city of Denver. There would be, for example, soft hot nights of playing baseball in the park and swimming in chilly lakes. Nevada was also to be a summer setting, with its relentlessly hot desert. *On the Road*'s autumn was in windy Chicago and St. Louis, the San Joaquin Valley, and lonely Indiana. Harsh winds slapping streetlamps and stirring leaves adrift beneath blazing sunsets. Lastly, winter's backdrop coated Butte, Montana, North Dakota, Portland, Oregon, and Idaho, all of which Kerouac witnessed firsthand. These notes, and dozens like them, reveal his constantly stirring and simmering an ever-evolving Crockpot of ideas.

Kerouac's outline of the novel of April 27, 1949, finally mirrored a semblance of sections of its final published form. He broke the book down into five sections, beginning with "Shades of the Prison House" in which Red Moultrie was to travel south from New York City on a Sunday evening in May, upon his release from prison. His first destination was Rocky Mount to get help from his "aunt."

The second section, the "beginning" of the pilgrimage, takes Moultrie to New Orleans before going to El Paso,

Texas, in search of Vern Pomeroy. Upon finding out that Vern is no longer there, he goes to Denver. However, Kerouac crossed out the last three cities and kept Moultrie moving west from Rocky Mount, ending up in Denver looking for Pomeroy. By then, Pomeroy has "moved on" with Moultrie hot on his tail through the states of Wyoming and Utah, and onward into Truckee, California. The end of the pilgrimage, the third section, takes place in San Francisco, where Moultrie finally finds Pomeroy and only then do they pursue "wild times" before beginning another quest, this time to find Pomeroy's father, Vern Sr.

The fourth section begins with Moultrie leaving Pomeroy in San Francisco and pursuing his fortune alone. He rides a bus to Portland, Oregon, and somehow finds his inheritance. In the last section, "The Valley Again," Moultrie ends up with his woman, Laura, goes to the Crossroads Bar in Denver, and, ultimately, disappears once more into an unnamed valley. It was, with some degree of certainty, the emergence of an American quest novel that Kerouac continued shaping, refining, deleting from and adding to. The magic of the book, he knew, was the idealization of a truly flawed character possessing a spark of divinity (like a man charged as an accomplice to a bank robbery, who prays over his Bible in a dank jail cell). Ultimately, Neal Cassady would fill that role as the evolving main characters transformed into thinly disguised biographical and autobiographical portraits. The only part that never changed was the certainty that America would always be the canvas on which anything could happen.

MY FELLOW GENIUSES

In a letter to Allen Ginsberg, dated March 15, 1949, Cassady whined that he had "broke his hand" shortly after his arrival with Kerouac. "I hit LuAnne with a left thumb to the forehead, caused an incomplete fracture of four bones about the base of the thumb." After a series of X-rays and twenty-one hours of various settings by a sympathetic doctor, Cassady was subjected to surgery. A steel pin was inserted beneath his thumbnail to provide traction and prevent a malformation. Cassady was certain now that he was permanently free of LuAnne, for he strove to remain focused on his "life's blood," his daughter, who left no doubt now that she was in need of a more permanent father. His other passion was musical. He was determined (barring any permanent handicap from his broken thumb) to learn to play the saxophone.

Ginsberg informed Cassady of Kerouac's "golden day," the much-earned acceptance of *The Town and the City* by Harcourt, Brace, that Kerouac was no longer "mad" at him for his behavior in San Francisco (and that five of the fifteen sandwiches that he denied to Cassady had in fact gone bad). As trivial as this was, it was a barometer of their friendship.

Burroughs was also in hot water. On April 6, while he was a passenger in a stolen car, a patrol car recognized the man with him. The police burst into Borroughs's home without a search warrant (thus fixing permanently every suspicion Burroughs would ever have about the law and government). As they were shaking him down, they found a trove of Burroughs's correspondence with Ginsberg, some of it thick with discussions of narcotics and homosexuality.

Burroughs warned Ginsberg on April 16 that the information was given to the "Feds," who were intent on questioning Burroughs "at length." He was charged with possession of narcotics and guns, threatened with the prospect of a two-to-five-year imprisonment in Angola State Prison (reputed to be one of the most dangerous in the nation), and the risk of a constant "shake-down" in the street as a known offender. Burroughs suspected that the police department had made a phone call to New York to inform them of Allen Ginsberg. Burroughs's concern was Ginsberg's co-occupants who were currently amassing a caché of stolen items in his apartment. For the moment, to avoid any problems related to drugs, Burroughs was "back on lush." By May, he and his family had moved back to Texas, living in a rented house in the town of Pharr.

Allen Ginsberg's apartment had turned into a halfway house for petty thievery. After Herbert Huncke turned up at his door, feet bloodied and blistered, unbathed, gaunt and starving, exuding misery, Ginsberg disregarded Burroughs's advice and offered Huncke a temporary stay in his York Avenue apartment. He nursed his old friend back to health. Huncke returned the favor, eventually, by stockpiling stolen merchandise with two other culprits, Little Jack Melody and Vicki Russell. Though Ginsberg never actively took part in this criminal activity, he was captivated, as he always had been, by the reckless lifestyle they all lived (Russell was also an ex-prostitute). Meanwhile, Burroughs's letters advised caution in regard to correspondence to and from himself, which Ginsberg habitually kept, as well as his personal journals. Ginsberg also thought it best to remove all the pilfered jewels, furs, coats, and a number of other things from the apartment.

They put it all in a car stolen in Washington, D.C., a few weeks before. Ginsberg, in need of a ride to his brother's house, put his journals and correspondence there as well. He sat in the backseat with Vicki Russell and a pile of clothing. Melody, on parole and without a license, drove down a one-way street on Forty-third Avenue in Long Island City. Melody panicked when he saw an idling patrol car and sped by the car (according to police, Melody also attempted to run down a police officer standing near the car), accelerating to sixty-five miles an hour, turning up 205th Street before spinning twice and ending upside-down. Everyone struggled out of the car. Melody and Russell were arrested. Ginsberg, dazed after losing his eyeglasses in the wreck, wandered back to his apartment.

Afterward, Ginsberg realized that his papers were still in the car, some with his home address. Anxious and desperate, he called Kerouac to ask if he was coming to his apartment that day and, if so, could he retrieve Ginsberg's other letters and journals and bring them to his place. Kerouac, copping out on his friend, said that his address was probably there as well and that they wouldn't be safe at his place either. He also added that if Ginsberg really wanted all of the material removed, he would have done so already. Disappointed, Ginsberg weakly agreed and hung up. Before long, the police arrived. Ginsberg and Huncke were arrested and jailed. During his arraignment, Ginsberg stated that he was among these criminal types to capture "realism" for his writing. He and Russell were held on a $2,500 bail. For Huncke and Melody, it was business as usual, and they ended up back in prison.

For his naive involvement in these affairs, Louis Ginsberg and some Columbia professors used their influence to have Allen committed for treatment at the New York State Psychiatric Institute in lieu of doing time in prison. Haunted by his own confusion, Ginsberg was optimistic for a "cure" and, influenced by Dostoevsky's *The Possessed,* which he had been reading, hoped that his "demons" would be "cast out." At the time, it gave Ginsberg a chance to reflect and respond to the crisis at hand.

Kerouac's reaction to all of this was to avoid involvement with Burroughs and Ginsberg since he was about to place himself into the public eye with *The Town and the City*'s publication. To Alan Harrington he expressed the chief difference between himself and his "fellow geniuses": "I am no longer 'beat,' I have money, a career. I am more *alone* than when I 'lurked' on Times Square at 4 A.M., or hitch-hiked penniless down the highways of the night." Unlike his notorious cohorts, Kerouac no longer thought himself as a rebel, but instead a "happy, sheepish imbecile, open-hearted & silly with joys." Furthermore, he felt little to no grief for Ginsberg, though he visited him at Bellevue.

This lack of empathy by Kerouac made him feel something had gone awry in his soul. Sitting on a river pier at Battery Park staring at the cool April water, he thought this was the moment to say "goodbye" to the city. With his new career as an established writer, Kerouac knew his next move should be to relocate himself and his family by June. New York no longer contained any "mystery" for him. Furthermore, his longing for a wife made him seriously consider returning to Edie Parker despite her family's obvious disdain for him.

Packing a bag of clothes and journals, Kerouac left before his mother and sister to obtain their new living quarters in Colorado. He would put his reckless past behind him and focus on his future; writer, rancher, wheat farmer, loyal son, husband, and father. His air of optimism was startling that spring, shining with a clarity he had never possessed before. It was a new but delusional house of cards that only required the slightest breeze for it all to come tumbling down.

THE SHROUDED STRANGER

Kerouac estimated that his move to Colorado would cost him around three hundred dollars. His family (with the exception of Paul Blake Sr., who was hesitant about being so far from his own family) was nervous but agreeable. Kerouac's initial plan was to hitchhike alone into the "red, red night." However, he ended up traveling by bus since it was both more expeditious and less troublesome. He was determined to be frugal and, by journey's end, he had only spent ninety cents on food. He rolled out of the depot that night, resonating from a lustful dalliance with Adele Morales only an hour before he boarded. At noon the following day, he roamed Pittsburgh before another bus took him to Chicago.

Mining towns and hills scarred by ruinous industrialization rolled past until he crossed the Ohio River, where the landscape began to noticeably improve. He struck up fleeting acquaintances with fellow passengers, including an aspiring young actor returning home to his father's grocery store. The bus crossed the Mississippi the next morning; wistful licks of May air breezed through the cracked windows. The smooth, pleasant journey through Missouri stifled Kerouac's doleful reveries of New York. The land turned greener: lush trees cast shadows over stirring vistas of grass. He could smell clover blended with freshly cut hay and the scent of rich loam boiling with springtime life. Kerouac enjoyed this part of the trip so much that he regretted the bus's imminent ascent into the High Plains.

In Marshall, Missouri, a "slatternly" woman got on the bus with her two children, one of whom sat on Kerouac's lap. Though the child never "budged an inch" or spoke, he held on firmly to Kerouac's hand "in perfect understanding that I was his good friend & father-like fellow traveler." There was a scent of rain, and darkening clouds soon boomed in a torrent of rain. It cleared shortly afterward, and the sky cast a rainbow over the Missouri River. Still intoxicated by the natural phenomenon of rivers and rain, Kerouac took advantage of a break when the bus reached Kansas City, Missouri. He walked the five miles to the confluence of the Kansas and Missouri rivers, located just below a railroad yard, where he noticed the high levees guarding the town.

Just before the next stop, the bus driver plowed into a cow. Though the rest of the passengers made obvious jokes about serving up steak, Kerouac was saddened as he signed a witness form for the driver: "an old white-faced cow, in its world of darkness, its rummaging, foraging, joyous, peaceful existence, doth cross the pavement of man from clover to sweetest clover—musing perhaps—and out of the dark comes the monster with the blazing eyes and the sign says 'Denver'—and WHAM!" In remorse, he composed a poem in his notebook about the cow.

Manhattan, Kansas, was dark, mysterious, brooding night-thoughts into an unblinking sky staying "*true* to its past." The bus, amid a "desert of night," stopped to transfer passengers to another bus. "Wild careening jalopies" sped dizzily past

Kerouac, driven by boys intoxicated by liquor and life. Again, scents appealed to him: the raw smell of the Kansas River, grilling hamburgers, burning cigarettes, and that "strangely haunting smell of gasoline in the air."

As the bus ascended the High Plains, Kerouac finally slept, his mind racing with dreams. About what, he did not know. Having forgotten them, he jotted down that "[s]omeday we'll all have died and nothing settled . . . just their forlorn rags of growing old." Kerouac put that statement almost intact into the closing paragraph of *On the Road.*

Dreams were not unusual during his trips. In the days before Ginsberg's arrest, Kerouac discussed his own dream of the "shrouded stranger." The idea of the stranger, according to Kerouac, arose from a dream he had of Arabia and Jerusalem. He was sauntering along a road curling west. A staff-carrying "Hooded Wayfarer" pursued him, casting behind it a slow "shroud of dust." To escape his pursuer, Kerouac knew he had to reach the "Protective City." His theory was that the shrouded stranger was "one's own self merely wearing a shroud." Ginsberg, who had composed a poem about this enigmatic figure, described it in a letter to Neal Cassady: "The important thing is that everybody has someone with deep socketed eyes and, or a green glassy visage, staring at him, in a crowd in a dream, of following him unseen in a desert, or seeking through the windowpane." In the end, the potent and allegorical figure found itself intact in *On the Road.*

By Sunday morning, after a smiling "blue-eyed cowboy" entered through the bus looking for a seat, Kerouac knew that he had finally reached the "True West." He struck up a conversation with the cowboy, who told him where to find fieldwork in Denver. Kerouac guessed the man was more "interested in mankind than 10,000,000 New School and Columbia professors and academicians." A likeness of the cowboy passenger stepping into a diner, all smiles and good cheer, can be found in part 1 of *On the Road*.

Thundershowers chased the bus into the Denver city limits. Kerouac wrote Hal Chase later that day that he had the feeling that he was "finding my world at last." As the rain broke, the sun "blushed" through some clouds over a section of brown land occupied by a solitary house. The farmhouse, as Kerouac conceived, was receiving "the blush of God Himself."

When he arrived, Kerouac called Justin Brierly after he was unable to track down Ed White. Brierly met him with a flashlight at the corner of Colfax Avenue and Broadway Street. That evening Kerouac rented a ten-cent room at the YMCA. Brierly gave him some Scotch to pass the night. In his cups, Kerouac wrote beaming letters of the joy of being in Denver at last. Three days later, he had rented a cottage in Westwood. In his element, he grilled sizzling steaks in the little yard while reading "cowboy stories." All he had to do for now was wait for his family to arrive.

THE SKELETON'S REJECTION

Kerouac had found a temporary job as a construction worker, which would begin later in the month. On his off-hours, he took long walks, read, and wrote. He began a new writing log determined to chart his progress, as he had done with his last novel. However, he found it difficult to leap into the work. The Western dime novels he avidly read helped to shape a new setting with convincing details. The genre, which could be traced back to James Fenimore Cooper's Leatherstocking series, usually had a series of action-packed sequences strung between a predictable narrative arc. Deadwood Dick, a character invented by Edward Wheeler, cemented the genre's popularity for readers young and old, into the twentieth century. The Western hero was young, handsome, and virile, always stood up for good and *always* got his girl. He was a gifted marksman and horseback rider, and defeated his enemies through blazing courage and honesty.

The ideal of the Western hero was also a self-made man rising from humble and obscure origins and lacking any formal education or inherited wealth. His success confirmed that obstacles could be overcome by a firm will to achieve and through individualism. The dime novels, Kerouac found, also contained authentic descriptions of the Western Plains, richly colored by sensory details. Otherwise, he felt his characterizations were ineffectively transparent. Though he wondered if his actual road novel would be any good, he accurately predicted its popularity.

Still, the real threat to Kerouac's temporary well-being was the prospect of being broke. Though it was a different situation now, because he had *some* money he could count on (though that too was contingent only upon the success of *The Town and the City*), by not making the right moves now, his financial situation could very well sour.

There was also what he referred to as the "Dark Corridor." One example was Ginsberg's "insanity," as construed by hospital psychiatrists, who were "curing" the poet of his homosexuality. The bright optimism of his new life was haunted by Ginsberg's incarceration and the guilt he felt at leaving his friend and comrade behind. Kerouac reasoned that Ginsberg was deliberately inventing his insanity to put himself in the same mental state as his mother, who was still institutionalized at Pilgrim State Hospital. Shrugging off the pessimism, he perceived a bright future for himself.

Spending time with friends Ed White and Frank Jeffries (Stan Shepard in *On the Road*), Kerouac admired how established they were. White had a house he built himself (with help from his friends). At the University of Denver, Kerouac watched Jeffries lecture a physics class. These people, Kerouac intuitively felt, *belonged* here. Again, the poisonous seeds of Kerouac's inadequacy began to sprout. Befriending a young boy (a "lost kid" he later thought) on a street, Kerouac accompanied him to a local amusement park. In the boy's company, Kerouac's sense of distance, his *separateness* from others, made him compare himself to Faulkner's character Joe Christmas from *Light in August*. Christmas, unable to both cope with the enigma of his mixed black-and-white heritage and to fit in anywhere in Faulkner's dysfunctional Yoknapatawpha County, resorts to murder before being slaughtered himself by a zealous racist. A kitten with damaged eyes reminded Kerouac of the child, lost and needy. A part of his depression came from his feeling that his family was wasting time arriving in Colorado. His self-esteem was slipping, his funds drained and, once again, he would appear to his family to be an utter failure. Furthermore, he had no furniture and no *typewriter*!

His spirits were revived by his love for horses. At a rodeo to which he accompanied the boy and his mother, Kerouac agreed to a fifteen-mile horseback ride. Before long, despite his saddle sores, he was running the horse as he held the reins, yipping with joy. The next day, he was too sore to take part in the rodeo. Back home, he was the subject of gossip about his friendship with the boy and his mother, originating, he thought, with an "old hen" next door peeking at him from behind her window shades.

On June 2 he received a telegram from his family saying that they planned on arriving in Denver that evening. Apart from the twenty dollars he was saving to plant the lawn (a condition of his rental contract), Kerouac was literally on his last penny. The timing was perfect. He was beginning to feel not only the pinch of poverty, but also the slow draining of his literary ambitions. No writing desk, no papers, no typewriter and, most importantly, no intellectual companionship of the vein of a Ginsberg or Burroughs.

The middle of June, with his family in place and normalcy restored, Kerouac typed ten thousand words more of his road novel. He was expecting his editor Robert Giroux to fly in on the fifteenth to begin the process of cleaning up *The Town and the City* for publication. However, the joy at working with his editor was stifled by his already disgruntled family, financial troubles, and a well that was drying up. Disgusted and miserable, gloom buried beneath the façade of joy he carried with him like empty baggage, he wrote a poem titled "The Skeleton's Rejection": "Roll your own bones, / go moan alone— / Go, go, roll your own bones, / alone. / Bother me no more."

ALONE

On the first of July, Gabrielle had had enough. She decided that she was too old for such a radical change and decided to return to her job in New York. On the Fourth of July, Kerouac, with Nin and her husband and son, accompanied Gabrielle to the Rock Island Railroad depot. It was, in Kerouac's estimation, one of the "saddest days" he had ever seen. To cheer up one another, they tried to picnic at Berkeley Lake. Shortly afterward, the Blakes went east behind her.

One Thursday evening, Kerouac stood in his yard watching heat lightning flicker over the eastern plains and, to the west, dancing across the mountain peaks. It held mystical associations for Kerouac for he felt that lightning in the East was more intense (equating it with the intense power of his New York experiences), yet the western lightning was "strangely wild," like San Francisco and Cassady. His desire was to leave Denver and go in both directions at once.

Robert Giroux had also come and gone, leaving Kerouac with the advice that he should leave novels like *Doctor Sax* alone and instead focus on real people. He had heard that advice before, from Pauline back in New York, who had also told him that his preoccupations with rain, rivers, and the formidable Sax were pointless ventures into profitless excess. There was "mush" in using too much symbolism and "private poetic myths" in novel writing. Giroux accurately sensed that Kerouac was influenced too much by Ginsberg's poetic visions.

Though Kerouac sometimes craved the idea of solitude, he did not like to be alone. He typed up a lengthy letter in response to Neal Cassady, urging him to be his pupil, to become a writer like himself. With his hopes for a royalty check in the fall, Kerouac wove a wild plan for them to unite and make money for themselves. Though he was desperate for cash and found a manual labor job at a fruit market, Kerouac wanted his "freedom." It went against his principals to punch a clock, to "stay out of trouble," as society wanted men to do. His proposal to Cassady was simple in its wording—to "revolutionize American letters."

Carolyn Cassady was five months pregnant with the child they planned on naming John Allen. Neal, undeterred by the rotten smell of his thumb, like a dying animal soft and sick beneath his hard cast, furiously one-armed heavy tires all day long at a garage. Daily, Carolyn injected him in the buttocks with penicillin to help ward off infection. The antibiotic gave him hives; the Fleming's juice he was also prescribed (a medicinal penicillin substance created after World War II by chemist Alexander Fleming, the creator of penicillin-producing mold), also gave him allergies. Codeine was prescribed to relieve the pain in his thumb, and his toe required surgery from a cystic inflammation. He was also suffering from a collapsed bridge in his nose from a past surgical attempt that had weakened the cartilage. To cap it off, the tip of his thumb had to be amputated. However, Cassady's plight was Kerouac's fortune. Kerouac later transplanted, almost verbatim, Cassady's vivid description (a clever act of outright plagiarism) of his latest turn of events into *On the Road*.

Cassady was also in the dark, almost four months after it happened, about Ginsberg's arrest. Ginsberg had not written of it, so Cassady asked Kerouac to supply the details. The letter excited Kerouac: not the contents of it, but the way it was written; seemingly effortless displays of alliteration and wordplay: "Frantic Frisco, yes, frenzied Frisco, yes, Fateful Frisco. Frisco of frivolous folly; Frisco of fearful fights. Frisco of Fossilization. Frisco: Fully Fashioned Fate." Cassady also alluded to film noir: "Wipe that smile off your face, this is murder, see? We're gonna catch the rat and you're gonna tell us where he is. Sam, bring the girl in here. All right, lady, this the guy?"

The letter was groundbreaking for Kerouac because of its confessional nature. Cassady spilled out his whole sordid past, his progression from petty theft to grand theft. This prompted Kerouac, who was not thinking of Carolyn's welfare, and their child and unborn baby, to advise him to drop his job, take up writing, and go to Paris with him once he received more money from Harcourt, Brace. As an alternative, Cassady invited Kerouac to San Francisco, where he and Carolyn had moved into a new home on Russell Street. It was all Kerouac could do to keep from packing his bag that instant and leave Denver as soon as possible. His glorious mythical West had sunk into a black hole of despair and disappointment, and it was time to move on.

By July 1949, Kerouac had already fashioned and refashioned a stable of characters into a story line that more or less maintained a flexible plot. The initial foray from the east coast to the west, traveling through cities like

Asheville, El Paso, Denver, North Platte, Central City, Truckee, and Lovelock, functioned merely as stopping points for the characters on the trail of *something* indefinable and elusive. The trip that initiated as a "pilgrimage" transformed into a spurious thread of "wild times"; ultimately aiming for redemption from the lingering haze of absolute *lostness*.

However, something was lacking. Underneath its naturalistic style of writing, the novel's foundation of search and redemption was a potent one. He knew he wanted to write this work differently than before, and that when it was finally accomplished, it would also be a novel that would break new ground. Kerouac's ultimate plan was to incorporate his life into a bildungsroman, a story detailing the feats of a hero spurred into journey, jarred into motion by personal loss, discontent, and alienation. In this respect, he shared the same aesthetic sensibility of novelist Saul Bellow, who, in *The Adventures of Augie March* (1953), espoused a World War II American picaresque.

Augie March's lead character endures a childhood through the Great Depression and blindly works his way through a variety of occupations, determined never to anchor himself at one place for any length of time. Bellow leaves the reader hanging by never revealing the character's objectives or destinations. Life for Bellow's March is a random crapshoot endured by day-to-day realities. Because the character considers commitment too constricting, his search broadens and expands. Though the novel cannot be considered an influence on Kerouac, it is a novel that boasts similar aspirations. The difference is that Bellow invented his story and characters; Kerouac drew them from real life.

The picaresque novel's hero, or sometimes antihero, rises from the lower rungs of his society. He depends on his wits to survive a society fraught with corruption and vice. Kerouac, having read Cervantes's *Don Quixote* and Mark Twain's *The Adventures of Huckleberry Finn* (Kerouac felt Twain equipped his characters with a "Missouri voice on a river pier") was very aware of the genre and the advantages it could bring to his writing.

Kerouac also felt that his writing *had* to shift stylistically from the syntax of *The Town and the City.* It needed more spontaneity. In *On the Road*'s later stages, the work slowly adopted a more confessional prose style, an approach reflected in a passage Kerouac once read in Goethe's *From My Life: Poetry and Truth.* Goethe wrote to a young author seeking advice, explaining the exact aesthetic that Kerouac saw as a way into a personal style he could call his own:

> He [the writer] does well with anything confined to inner experience, feeling, disposition and reflections on these; and he will deal successfully with any theme where they are treated. But he has not yet developed his powers in connexion with anything

> really objective. Like all young men, nowadays, he rather fight shy of reality, although everything imaginative must be based on reality, just as every ideal must come back to it. The theme I set this young man was to describe Hamburg as if he had just returned to it. The thread of ideas followed from the start was the sentimental one of his mother, his friends, their love, patience and help.

Kerouac set out to emulate Goethe's design. "I remembered [. . .] Goethe's admonition, Goethe's prophecy that the future literature of the West would be confessional in nature."

Kerouac's confessional and spontaneous style began to take hold in *On the Road,* paving the way for other works that similarly maintained this firm aesthetic: "You simply give the reader the actual workings of your mind during the writing itself: you confess your thoughts about events in your own unchangeable way . . . did you ever hear a guy telling a long wild tale to a bunch of men in a bar and all are listening and smiling, did you ever hear that guy stop to revise himself, go back to a previous sentence to improve it, to defray its rhythmic thought impact . . . he's passed over it like a part of the river that flows over a rock once and for all and never returns and can never flow any other way in time?"

Perhaps forgetting the earnest jottings he placed in his

1947–48 journals about the exciting process of writing *The Town and the City,* he asserted that he had "spent my entire youth rehashing, speculating and deleting and got so I was writing one sentence a day and the SENTENCE had no feeling. Goddamn it, FEELING is what I like in art," he told interviewers from *The Paris Review* in the summer of 1968, "not CRAFTINESS and the hiding of feelings." Most importantly, imagination ultimately took a back seat to experience, as suggested by Goethe, which perhaps explains why Kerouac's early stabs at formulating a plot and character development for *On the Road* never firmly solidified:

> A writer needs experience. Some writers need it more than others. I couldn't be a writer without it, because I couldn't sit down and make up fairy tales. I'd be a faker. But then experience without the ability to write, without education that is, is no good either; because you couldn't write about your experience, and you'd be just a bash nosed drunk like any other bash nosed drunk who tried to express himself in a bar. Nobody would give a shit. But then again, if one could write but had no experience he'd be like Mr. Milquetoast looking up anxiously from his tome, or waving his umbrella at butterflies." (*Visions of Cody,* 178)

There was, however, a certain inherent risk by the close of the 1940s that Kerouac either ignored or he was ignorant of. The threat of Communism in the United States, sparked by a zealous Joseph McCarthy and his list of 250 suspected Communists in the United States State Department, made writers, artists, politicians, and even the average Joe on the street, anybody displaying a semblance of eccentricity, automatically suspect. Changes in the world's makeup stoked red coals of fear: China's falling to Mao, the Soviet Union's development of the atomic bomb, and Soviet spy Klaus Fuchs's confession poured gasoline upon McCarthy's escalating fiery campaign of hate. Kerouac's frankness concerning drugs, homosexuality, interracial relations, and sex certainly provided an edge to what he was writing at this time. One could reasonably assume that he maintained an idealistic holdover from the early 1940s, a belief in Russia's "universal brotherhood of man."

Though he knew the path he vowed to follow with his writing, the work remained as fluctuating ideas in his journal. For the moment he was concerned with his immediate needs. Kerouac left Denver because his fantasy of a communal ranch family (his own and the Cassady's) had been dashed to pieces. Carolyn Cassady recalls:

> Jack was always looking for a home. Perhaps, the homestead/ranch idea evolved from his fascination with the WEST. It later evolved into one big house for

> us all in Mexico. In his letters to me, whenever he'd run across a house he liked, he'd describe it in detail, knowing I loved old big houses as he did. Letters between him and Neal elaborated on the ranch idea. Neal even sent off for pamphlets about land rights and all that. I was so disappointed none of their big plans ever materialized." (Correspondence with author, Sept. 29, 2006)

Kerouac was at a crossroads, personally and creatively. His friends were scattered now like blown rose petals across the dark wine spill of America. For once, he was on his own, or so it seemed. In a touching passage from *Visions of Cody,* Kerouac evoked the depth of his disappointment at this time: "So I died, I died in Denver I died; I said to myself, 'What's the use of being sad because your boyhood is over and you can never play softball like this; you can still take another mighty voyage and go and see what Cody is finally doing.'" The feeling of "lostness" was inescapable, a bleeding wound, "nothing in the world matters; not even success in America but just void and emptiness awaits the career of the soul of man." Kerouac remembered walking across a wide sandy field after watching Bob Giroux's plane leave from the Denver airport, feeling a "sad red speck on the face of the earth." Denver had turned into a caustic dose of reality: "I came to the streets of Denver in their infinitely soft, sweet and delightful August evening; dusk it was, I say, purple, with shacks in soft alleys, and many lawns, all over Denver're many lawns all the time." Walking unworried about getting lost, as he used to do in Lowell, he envied others for being at ease with themselves: women leaning on bright porches clutching giggling children or telling their man a secret best kept in the security of the bedroom, raucous laughter from a dirty joke, the innocent glee of children playing ball in the sunset. Kerouac felt that he was not, *could* not, be a part of any of this.

The lights of a softball field glowed under the looming moon. A game was in progress, and women and men were cheering from the bleachers. Life went on, both foreign and distant from Kerouac standing on its sidelines. It was Cassady's field from his youth where he caught fly balls; it was Denver's field, not Kerouac's. Not even comfortable in his own skin, Kerouac's sense of being an outcast took hold. Indecision gripped him, and, mired between assuming responsibility or following the often misguided advice of his spirit, he chose to do what he had always done when he was unable to resolve matters on his own. He simply left.

"POINTING STRAIGHT AT ME"

He sat in the backseat of a travel bureau car, a 1949 Ford, with his head against the window watching the countryside sweep along once again. He enjoyed the notion that for the price of eleven dollars he had no responsibility; he didn't have to talk or respond when spoken to (as he felt compelled to do when he was offered a ride during hitchhiking), all he had to do was sit and absorb the rise and fall of the arid western lands under the skies strewn with cumulus clouds, an impression he embellished upon in a written passage that he famously read on *The Steve Allen Show* in 1959:

> At the junction of the state line of Colorado, its arid western one, and the state line of poor Utah I saw in the clouds huge and massed above the fiery golden desert of eveningfall the great image of God with forefinger pointed straight at me through halos and rolls and gold folds that were like the existence of the gleaming spear in His right hand, and sayeth, Go thou across the ground; go moan for man; go moan, go groan, go groan alone go roll your bones, alone; go thou and be little beneath my sight; go thou, and be minute and as a seed in the pod, but the pod the pit, world a pod, universe a pit; go thou, go thou, die hence; and of Cody report you well and truly.

His midnight arrival in San Francisco was unannounced. With bag in hand, he stood at the front door of Cassady's house.

Cassady was anxiously awaiting Kerouac's arrival for reasons of his own. He wanted to, *had* to, leave the claustrophobic confines of Russell Street. Though he loved his wife and daughter, and looked forward to the imminent arrival of their child, he didn't like to be restrained from enacting the exciting possibilities his impulsive nature envisioned. Because Cassady's railroad work had dried up, Carolyn got an office job before learning she was pregnant (despite being on birth control at the time) with a child she wasn't altogether sure she actually wanted, at least with her husband.

Carolyn and Cassady heard a knock at the door as they lay in bed, and he, "in the altogether," answered the door. Carolyn remembered years later in her memoir of the period that the "old familiar fear crept over me. I imagined a drawbridge between me and Neal being drawn up, enclosing them in their castle of delights and leaving me sitting wistfully on the opposite bank, filling the moat with tears." She heard them, excited, whispering and shuffling around downstairs oblivious to the family trying to sleep.

Carolyn cooked dinner and treated Kerouac congenially, despite her suspicions that he enabled Cassady's irresponsible behavior. After they finished, they leapt up and went out the door. Sensing her growing disapproval and annoyance, Cassady invited her out for a fun Saturday night. Carolyn's memory of the night was of being a "fifth wheel." The car slowed to a crawl in San Francisco's Fillmore district and came to a stop. Cassady leapt out the car into doorways, hunting for some pot. Eventually, the car was parked along a darkened residential district for a long, uneventful wait. They then moved on to the squalid Tenderloin district, home to an abundance of seedy bars, rundown hotels, and an abundant multiethnic populace.

Kerouac sat with Carolyn while Cassady hunted for a score. Later, jaded strippers moved languidly on a nightclub stage while Carolyn, barely entertained, sat mum. Neal returned and at once flirted with a woman on the stage, mortifying Carolyn so much that she wanted to go home. He dropped her off and did not return until the following morning.

Kerouac and Cassady came back to the house the next day with Henri Cru in tow. Cru, watching Carolyn bathe her daughter, remarked what a "charming domestic scene" it was. When Cru followed Kerouac back to the kitchen, Carolyn burst into tears, wishing that her life was what Cru assumed it was. Cru and Kerouac went outside; Cassady went upstairs with an air of frivolity, unmindful of the misery he was inflicting upon his wife. He "showered" her with "pretty, empty endearments." Carolyn's response was the only weapon she had, with her teeth clenched: "Get—out! Just go—just get *out*!" Puzzled, he responded, "All right, dear—I'm going."

That night, Carolyn slept fitfully. At dawn she heard the familiar soft patter of feet outside her bedroom door. After Kerouac ascended to the attic bedroom, Cassady prepared to step into bed. However, Carolyn blocked him from opening the blankets and lying next to her. Sticking to her guns, she again told him to leave and to take Kerouac with him. If this was the path he was determined to follow, she reminded him, then so be it. Instead of putting up a fight, Cassady opened an old battered suitcase and began filling it with clothes. He casually dressed, then went upstairs to retrieve Kerouac. Even before the stillness of the house began to envelop her, she realized that for practical purposes, she had made a mistake.

THE HOLY GOOF

The two men needed a car, so Cassady immediately thought of Helen Hinkle and her neighbor, Lorraine, who he knew owned one. Knocking on Helen's door, he said they were on their way to New York and that they needed a place to keep their belongings. They asked her if they could shower in her place. She agreed. The next morning, as Helen later repeated to Carolyn, Jack told Helen that Carolyn had kicked them both out of the house, as if to justify Cassady's departure from his family.

At the time, Helen was alone—Al had the traveling bug Cassady had infected him with and had left. Her dislike for Cassady was as strong as her growing admiration for Jack. She took the pair in for a night. Kerouac testified to Helen castigating Neal in both *On the Road* and *Visions of Cody.*

Despite the friction, Helen and Lorraine decided to go

out with Cassady and Kerouac to some jazz joints in the Fillmore section. In a jazz club on Howard Street, an exuberant Cassady, high on marijuana, stood in front of the saxophone swaying his body, sweating profusely, grooving to the beat of the bop rhythms. He asked Helen and Lorraine, sitting on their bar stools, "Can you dig it? Can you dig it?" It was frantic, and, in Kerouac's opinion, the "greatest day" of Cassady's life.

Afterward, the men split to Oakland to score more weed. The girls planned on rendezvousing with them at Jackson's Nook. Jackson's Nook was one of nearly two dozen black-owned jazz venues spread around the Fillmore during the 1940s. The cream of the crop of jazz musicians arranged side trips to the Fillmore district to jam with local musicians such as Duke Ellington, Charles Mingus, Louis Armstrong, Billie Holiday, Miles Davis, and Dexter Gordon, among many others, made regular appearances there. It was an evening Kerouac remembered fondly—a "night of Frisco jazz at its rawest peak"—that he made it a running thread in both *On the Road* and *Visions of Cody.* The music, so caustic, so raw, and so determined to break through to another level of consciousness, was a display of the furthest extreme of bop. It was beyond merely reaching and sustaining the highest note, but of obtaining "IT," an assimilation of soul and spirit spit out in its purest form through the notes of a horn, the peaks of creative writing, or in pure, spirited conversation.

The next morning, Cassady collected his suitcase and

Kerouac's bag from Helen Hinkle. She was shocked, she later told Carolyn, that he was deserting his family. Pushing his luck even further, Cassady convinced Helen, because he had a bad hand, to write a farewell note to Carolyn. The note, written on the back of a 1947 calendar, was dropped off at Carolyn's work. In this cowardly missive, her husband told her that he was leaving and that he would never bother her again. He left for her troubles three dollars, promising to send more by the next month.

Neal Cassady, to his immense relief, was off again, forging a new chapter in his life to be included in *On the Road* and *Visions of Cody*: "His wife threw him out just as I got there and only because it was a climactic moment, and we bowled back to the East Coast in a trip that was so frantic and so crazy that it has a beginning, and an end," Kerouac wrote several years later in *Visions of Cody*.

THE FATHER NEVER FOUND

The "Great Voyage" began with another travel bureau car, this time a 1948 Plymouth making a familiar trek for Kerouac and Cassady: back to Denver. This time they were not looking for LuAnne, or any other woman, but for Cassady's father. In the car with them were some tourists on their way to Sacramento, California. They carried on an excited banter, more and more daringly candid, until it elicited a complaint from the driver of the car, who they later found out was a "pansy." During the drive, Kerouac found out from Cassady that they shared the vision, while driving or riding in a car, of having a great scythe in hand and sweeping it along the countryside, slicing everything in half.

Their mutual imaginative forays also extended into a claustrophobic Sacramento hotel room where Cassady charmed the driver into bed and had his way with him. Kerouac, either scared, thrilled, intrigued, or a combination of all three, hid in the bathroom, watching: "That night the gangbelly broke loose between Cody and the skinny skeleton, sick: Cody thrashed him on rugs in the dark, monstrous huge fuck, Olympian perversities, slambanging big sodomies that made me sick, subsided with him for money; the money never came. He'd treated the boy like a girl!" (Visions of Cody, 358). At one point Kerouac cracked open the bathroom door and saw Cassady holding up the man's legs "like a dead hen" over his shoulders. This, a sickened Kerouac felt, was out of character for Cassady now that he was living a "workingman's life and marriage." The account of this made it into the scroll version of *On the Road,* but was later excised from the manuscript.

The next day, Cassady drove, his thumb bandage partially unraveled, while that same hand gripped the wheel with uncanny precision. Kerouac noticed, as if it were a barometer gauging their ragged travels, that the bandaged thumb got dirtier and dirtier as they went further east. Picking up the pace now, the pedal to the floor, Cassady stared straight ahead while the others bitched at how reckless and fast he drove. They flew through Donner Pass, that long stretch of desolation Kerouac had first seen three years before. The interior of the car was now thick with tension. Having to share the travel bureau car with strangers put a crimp on their conversation though Cassady remained undaunted. Kerouac sensed the stark differences between himself and Cassady and the others; he and his renegade subject represented, in their wild eagerness, the "vicious novelties of America."

The broad expanse of Salt Lake, stark and flat within its basin of earth, ribboned the horizon with a dim shimmer. Cassady was sleeping in the backseat next to Kerouac, who was trying to nod off. He overheard the people talking in the front seat, that he and Cassady were simply "cha-rac-ters" bent on making their comfortable bourgeois lives miserable, ruining an otherwise perfect trip across the American West. By the time darkness fell, the car entered Neal Cassady's birthplace—Salt Lake City, Utah.

While the others dined in a restaurant, the two men walked the streets. Kerouac remembered his 1947 trip through the city. He saw the spot where he watched two white children and one black child with his dog whittling sticks on the train tracks, and the place where he slept on the sparse lawn of a gas station. Quickly, with no time to waste

(Kerouac stated that it was *their* time that the others were eating up), they all loaded back into the car for the final leg of the trip to Denver. Between Salt Lake City and Denver, he felt the true restless spirit of Neal Cassady's upbringing dwell like an infernal fire brooding in the hearth of the earth. At Colorado's Green River, Cassady took the wheel so that the others could sleep in the backseat.

They were "hungup" in Denver for "various reasons" and moved on, foregoing the search for Neal Cassady Sr. to arrive in New York City sooner. The truth was that Neal Jr. was up to his old escapades again, perhaps sparked by the awful memories of his Denver youth as the "Barber's Boy." In West Alameda, he tossed pebbles at the bedroom window of a schoolgirl Kerouac knew ("she had nice goose pimples on her knees," says Kerouac in *Visions of Cody*). Instead, her mother answered him with a shotgun leveled over her arm. At a carnival, Cassady was hot on the trail of a preteen Mexican girl before being distracted by yet someone else. His morals gone, Cassady was like an infectious plague.

Somehow, word got to Kerouac's family what he was up to. Phone calls home brought accusations from his incensed family that he was a home wrecker and was "harboring criminals." Cassady, staying true to his reputation, kept busy stealing cars for the remainder of the night. Exhausted with Cassady's antics and hungover from drinking Old Grandad, Kerouac fell asleep on the lawn of a Lutheran church. While he slept, Cassady "conned" a naive waitress. Picking her up in the Caddy with vague promises of marrying her after he returned back east, he used the satanic charm of a snake-oil salesman. Easing her into the spacious backseat, he fucked and ditched her like he did the spoiled handkerchief he used to wipe himself with. Desperately, she told Cassady as he was leaving that she was willing to follow him, if she had to, to New York. She never saw him again.

The car's owner, a "millionaire," needed his 1947 Cadillac limousine taken to Chicago. Foolishly, without any references, he was willing to let Kerouac and Cassady take the car as long as they paid for their own gas. With the latter at the wheel, they left behind Denver, Cassady's sordid past, and his stepbrother Jack Daly, who only a day earlier had tried to get Cassady to sign papers to have him and his alcoholic father, *wherever* he was, relinquish any claim on the Daly family's property. Two paying customers, a pair of Irish Jesuit college boys, got in and, before long, the car was aimed for Chicago, with a target arrival of the following evening.

Speeding for as hard and long as the Cadillac could hold out, sometimes reaching speeds of 110 miles per hour, Cassady jetted along the blacktop roads with focused determination until the car's brakes and rods rapidly wore down. At one point, he went more than a hundred miles out of his way to see Ed Uhl's ranch, where he had spent part of his youth riding horses and working. Even that was not without its complications; Cassady's speeding in the night rain along a muddy stretch of road threw the car into a ditch. As Cassady left to find help in the pouring rain, the trembling boys in the back seat asked an angry Kerouac if Cassady was his brother, adding, "He's crazy."

Soliciting the help of a farmer with a tractor who charged them five dollars for his services, the Cadillac, now irreparably damaged, was extracted from the thick mud. Undaunted, Cassady "balled the jack" of the car, causing flinty pebbles from the road to smack viciously off of the fender. Another fender-bender in Des Moines caused a two-hour delay in a police station. At one point, Cassady drove straight toward the grille of an oncoming semi-trailer truck in order to pass a line of cars, before deftly swerving back into his own lane. This truly terrified Kerouac, who, more than ever, recognized the complete psychosis of his friend.

They picked up two hitchhiking hoboes, who they charged fifty cents for gas, and they reached Chicago by dusk. They cruised the city for women, unsuccessfully. They took in some jazz at the Loop seeing again their "God," blind George Shearing, tearing it up at the piano once more. Later, they parked the car where they were supposed to and boarded a bus for Detroit.

In Detroit, Kerouac and Cassady walked to Grosse Pointe to visit Edie Parker. Having no place to sleep, they decided to do so on her parents' property. When a patrol car arrived, they went to a movie theater to kill time until

Edie freed herself. This time, Kerouac saw Edie without interference from her mother, but the occasion was less than auspicious. The Edie of New York had moved on with her life, more or less stabilized by the presence of her family, having her own car, and a steady source of income. She never looked at Kerouac "seriously" he thought, despite his hard-won accomplishment of being a published writer at last. At last, Edie left, making him and Cassady walk four miles back to the city. Neal and Jack found another car to complete their journey, this time a gleaming Chrysler driven by an agreeable man who offered to drive them for next to nothing.

Once in New York, filthy and bedraggled, Cassady and Kerouac saw less of each other. For better or for worse, though again Cassady had disappointed Kerouac, he had given the writer new ideas for *On the Road*. The trip to New York and the events preceding it in San Francisco ultimately found their way into the 1951 version of *On the Road* and into *Visions of Cody*. Kerouac wrote up an inventory of the usable material from this experience: "the jazz in Frisco, the trip in the Gag Plymouth, the Talk in the Backseat, Salt Lake City & Neal's broken thumb bandage, Denver, the Carnival night, Ed Uhl's ranch in Sterling, the Cadillac Limousine to Chicago, Detroit, the Chrysler to New York."

THE PHANTOM OF DESIRE

Kerouac's return to New York City in late August 1949 hosted a wrenching drunken crawl through the city bars while enduring the arduous process of reediting *The Town and the City* with Robert Giroux. The experiences of the past few weeks still rang a sharp, persistent chord within him. He had, for now, his fair share of America. Lastly, he was planning to complete his road novel in Paris, when and if he ever got there. So far, Italy with Cassady was a no-go. All of his money was spent and he was anchored, to his avail, at his mother's new apartment in Richmond Hill, Long Island.

Kerouac was caught between his responsibilities with his publisher and his renewed urge to write. His thoughts returned to *Doctor Sax* and *On the Road* before putting down both for a few days. He picked up the latter again and retitled it *Hip Generation*. What is hip? Dawn-choked cities with rain-slicked streets; dusky nightclubs smoking bebop jazz from its darkened doorways; jaded hipsters slinking at dawn's break, escorting broken-hearted hookers. But it still didn't gel. Composing new continuity inserts for *The Town and the City* clouded his thoughts for *Hip Generation* and he again set it aside. What he felt now was ambiguity. Edie's refusal to accept him back into her life, Cassady's raging and blatant criminality, and his own paranoiac unease blunted his stoic determination to succeed. For some reason, he determined now that simple living, even though life itself was a holy entity, was not enough. Almost in wonderment, the "first time in years," the twenty-six-year-old Kerouac did not know how to proceed with his life or his fiction.

INEZ

Cassady knew exactly how to proceed after spending only a few days in Richmond Hill with Gabrielle and Kerouac (wisely, Gabrielle did not want Cassady staying there any longer). Cassady needed a new con, a new way out. She was, as Kerouac described her in *Visions of Cody*, a "raving fucking beauty." Twenty-five-year-old Diana Hansen (Inez in part 4 of *On the Road*) was a fashion model and an aspiring writer in New York City. Dark-haired and beautiful, she was the type to fall exactly for a man like Neal Cassady. They first met at a party through Allen Ginsberg and, not long afterward, Cassady moved into her apartment on East Seventy-fifth, the "slums," according to Kerouac.

Carrying on the life of a smooth sophisticate, in a silken robe and a perpetual marijuana cigarette dangling from his mouth, Cassady had finally hit his personal jackpot. Here was a chance for him to start anew, to redefine himself with a sensible lifestyle. For all he knew, Carolyn had ejected him from the house and this time meant it, which left him a free agent as far as womanizing was concerned. However, he still had a child to support and, immediately, he got himself a job parking cars to do that and to help pay rent. Sometime in the ensuing months he and Diana conceived a child.

Days with Kerouac continued to excel; at Bop City they listened to Lionel Hampton and George Shearing. To encourage Cassady's writing, Kerouac obtained for him a typewriter from Harcourt. Other times, they both huddled by the wood stove in Cassady's parking lot shack, discussing life, girls, writing, and literature.

Meanwhile, Kerouac managed to live it up on the short editor/author honeymoon period between him and Robert Giroux. Dining on steaks with the Harcourt salesmen, drinking with Giroux at the bar in the Waldorf, pinballed Kerouac from business to leisure. "Meanwhile," he wrote in his journal, "*On the Road* is on the road, that is, moving." He began toying with the idea of a new character, or rather an old one transformed now into "Dean Moriarty." He visualized his new character, a stand-in for Neal Cassady, standing before a movie poster and pointing at a screen actress lounging upon it; "Look at that belly!" Kerouac imagined that if his new character ever actually met this woman, he would "clam up in awe of this awesome world." He would blurt out, enraptured: "Think of all the things between that broad and me! Miles of people, agents, nightclubs, producers, money, right connections! Yet how I would love her, every hidden bit!—as no man ever *dared*!"

The war-torn decade of the 1940s was coming to a close. The next would be a decade of optimism replete with rock'n'roll, drive-in theaters, bobby socks, and James Dean. By and large, it was the end of an era for Kerouac. The next seven years would test his endurance as a writer harshly. Though he would finally be published in March 1950, it came to nothing in the end. All he had, all he *still* had, was the ragtag bits and pieces of his road novel.

On August 25, 1949, Kerouac began anew the opening pages of *On the Road*. The story was to begin in Colorado in the year 1928. A two-hundred-acre farm is labored over by Old Wade Moultrie's son, Smiley, and Vern Pomeroy. When some "hoodlums" steal Old Wade's Ford, Wade pulls a gun on them and shoots to kill. However, the newest direction of the novel was nothing more than a creative misfire. Kerouac attempted to instill the Old West in another mythic figure that did more to confuse the story than bring it imaginative breadth. The first week of September saw Kerouac re-titling the novel once again. "Official Log of the Hip Generation" staggered on for eighteen pages depicting "Shades of the Prison House," something he had attempted a week earlier. This time, Mary Moultrie, the mother of Red was involved in sexual relations with Dean Pomeroy. She gives birth to Dean Pomeroy, Jr., and subsequently dies. The farm dissipates after Wade dies, an analogy that illustrates Kerouac's intention of bringing the days of the Old West to a close. All this work was Kerouac's method of arriving at the pith of the story; it wasn't a solution. By September 29, Kerouac admitted to himself that he was stuck: "For the first time in years I DON'T KNOW WHAT TO DO. I SIMPLY DO NOT HAVE A SINGLE REAL IDEA WHAT TO DO."

CHAPTER SEVEN

SPRING IN NEW YORK

Kerouac attempted *On the Road* once again in November 1949. After drawing a map of America, he this time wanted the novel to begin in a New York jail before journeying to New Orleans, northern California, Montana, Denver, and resolving itself in New York City's Times Square. New characters came into play beside old ones, most notably "Old Bull" and "Marylou."

By the spring of 1950, Kerouac was restless to move on and leave the city. He found his work of late to be nothing less than "ragged and sad." To continue receiving money from the government, he found someone to sign for him that he was attending classes. Writing to Ed White in January 1950, Kerouac detailed at length what he longed for as the month of his birth approached: "In March I begin to smell what must be going on in the great Missouris and Yellowstones and even Yukon rivers of the north—a muddy exhalation of the earth which in summer becomes like a tropical isle of vales—and I gotta go."

He was also seeking White's assistance in finding out some geographical details of rivers and floods "inundating the big cities." Recalling his own experience of crossing on the Algiers Ferry, he had Red Moultie peer over the rails and watch the logs floating down the Mississippi River coming from "Montana, where his father is." The details were once again tied together, a bundle of ideas waiting to be utilized correctly in his road novel: "Rainy nights, hitch-hiking; rivers; floods; states, towns; bop in niggertowns; freights; the plains—and hoboes singing: 'Home in Missoula, home in Truckee, home in Opelousas, but ain't no home for me. Home in Old Medora, home in Wounded Knee, home in Ogallala, home I'll never be, home I'll never be'" (JK to Ed White, January 28, 1950).

More ideas fell into place for his road novel. He realized that the novel would be his vehicle in which he could display his skills as a lyric poet, a street prophet, and a "possessor of a responsibility to my own personality." Kerouac's intentions were an "indescribable sad music of the night in

America." Beyond the notion of using bop jazz as his inspiration, his idea plunged deeper, beyond literal sound; it was also the figurative "inner" sound of the country itself. He detected a noise sounding from the "void"; a plaintive cry from humanity, arousing in him the feeling that man does not inhabit the earth, that he "haunts" it:

> More than a rock in my belly, I have a waterfall in my brain; a rose in my eye, a beautiful eye; and what's in my heart but a mountainside, and what's in my skull: a light. And in my throat a bird. And I have in my soul, in my arm, in my mind, in my blood, in my bean a grindstone of plaints which grinds rock into water, and the water is warmed by fires, and sweetened by elixirs, and becomes the pool of contemplation of the dearness of life. ("Notes of 1950 February" from *Windblown World,* 262)

When Kerouac received the first few advance copies of his new book on January 23 and began sending them out to some of his close friends, it was a pivotal moment. He wondered if the novel's release would send him to the poorhouse or a mansion. If it was fame he was acquiring, he was ready for it. As for obscurity, he already had it. Either way, he could not lose. All he had to do was merely adapt, realizing that the new year would be a landmark one for him.

Determined, he fixed a schedule for writing to show

Giroux, once he returned from Italy in February. If the book took off, he would postpone his western trip (for which he had already obtained a new atlas map). Optimistically, he hoped to have over fifty thousand words before his return. However, this plan collapsed under the weight of the constant social obligations he took on in order to court the novel to the American public. He also took in an abundance of jazz: the new Birdland club to hear the moody broodings of Miles Davis and Lennie Tristano, Bop City to absorb the ebullience of Dizzy Gillespie. When Tristano was exploring his more radical abstract forays in his signature song "Intuition," Kerouac heard an audience member shout, "Play some music!" Tristano, who had dropped formal composition and any prearrangements of harmony, rhythm, or melody in favor of free-flowing improvisation, was a harbinger of the free jazz form that came later. Kerouac agreed with the heckler, feeling that any art form will die when it sought to describe "itself" instead of "life." In the coming years, he would contradict this when he sought to free himself totally from conventional narrative in favor of the spontaneous prose form. He, like Tristano and others, would receive his own critical lambasting after the publication of such works as *Mexico City Blues* and *Old Angel Midnight*.

The novel's formal publication in March 1950, the month Kerouac turned twenty-eight, was greeted with some respectable reviews, with nods to Thomas Wolfe, though even the *New York Times* was aware of the spiritual scope that framed the novel and of Kerouac's technical virtuosity. Others, like his hometown newspaper, the *Lowell Sun,* called the book "an unpleasant story [. . .] with language often profane and vulgar." Dismissing that review as the work of provincials, Kerouac also ignored reviews that, he thought, were written by third-rate unpublished writers. He knew himself that *The Town and the City* had its share of influences, but he wished that his work would be stylistically appreciated as that of *Jack Kerouac*. Even as *The Town and the City* sold sluggishly, Kerouac believed that the novel that would truly make his name was *On the Road*.

Despite his moroseness, Kerouac's friends and acquaintances appreciated the fact that his hard work had finally paid off, at least with publication. Ginsberg was especially awed, as he realized that an author's life was an obtainable goal and worthy of life's sacrifice. Kerouac's taste of it included being introduced as an "author" at parties, accompanying his editor to social functions, being introduced to Carl Sandburg—who told Kerouac that he was just like him, a "hobo," though he sat in opera balconies dressed as he would never dress again, formal, sharp, and clean. He created a new lifestyle for himself on paper: chin-ups from the door, black coffee, less time sleeping, two meals a day instead of three, and to lose some of the weight he had gained from excessive food and drink. He even extended this positive outlook to his prose, to "express" more and "record" less, to show feelings instead of simply documenting the American panorama that had awed him for the last two years. In his tailored suit, Kerouac was all self-assurance and confidence, despite the miasma of nervous anxiety that continued to gnaw at him.

By April 1950, sales had slowed to a trickle and the publisher had ceased advertising it as a new selection. This, he knew, would reduce the royalty check he was counting on for his next trip to Denver. Predictably, Kerouac's impulse was to blame the publisher in general, and Giroux specifically, for the many deletions exacted upon *The Town and the City,* something he vowed never to allow again. The irony of the whole thing was stifling; four years of putting aside the "joys of normal youthful life" to make a "serious" contribution to American literature were all for naught. The result, in his estimation, was that *The Town and the City* was being treated by book reviewers, who did the same thing day after day with other books, as a "cheap first novel." If critics perceived characters like the doomed Alexander Panos, the visionary Leon Levinsky and the Job-like George Martin as frivolous, and if they expected from their books a proper social array of intellectuals, how would they treat his "miserable" new hitchhiking road characters?

Kerouac's latest love interest (not just a crush but one he felt that he actually "fell in love with") was Sara Yokeley, a beautiful and enigmatic woman who worked days as a UPI (United Press International) editor. She had attracted attention in

1944 by winning the Ernest H. Abernathy Award. Having worked for a while in the lower echelons of journalism, she was now an independent woman. Sometimes she took Kerouac with her on news assignments. He thought of proposing marriage to her because he felt that they shared commonalities. He was anxious to move on with his life, to place himself with his more sophisticated friends, imagining himself like Faulkner, writing important novels within the cloisters of Rowan Oak.

Sara's eagerness to cook for Kerouac and go to baseball games with him made her seem like perfect marriage material. However, Lucien Carr, who had dated her before Kerouac did, was trying to win her back. She toyed with the notion of being Kerouac's wife, especially after Twentieth-Century Fox showed interest in *The Town and the City.* However, both Sara and the movie studio went nowhere and, once again, Kerouac felt himself a "failure" in love and careerlike aspirations.

Kerouac was hopeless to improve their relationship. He confused her streak of independence with haughtiness. After their relations collapsed, the city was nothing more than a harsh mirror reflecting his constant misery. Kerouac took to the notion of going on the road, sooner than later. It was an easy and accessible solution, one he pursued when he felt "loveless." It was like moving onto another life. He remained hopeful that he would meet his "new wife" someday, *somehow.* In addition to Denver, he also made plans to travel to Mexico for the first time, to see William Burroughs, who had expatriated himself from the United States. In the back of his mind, he saw himself working in Denver and then moving on to Mexico for some other miscellaneous job. Yet he confessed to his journal that he would do neither. He would only end up spending more money and wasting his time.

One day after smoking some pot, Kerouac had a hallucinatory vision of his dead brother Gerard and, over the next two weeks, the ghostly specter coached him on his immediate life issues. One afternoon he imagined a conversation debating the merits and demerits of the road. Gerard's response was sarcasm: "Go away," be a "fool." When he returned, he would only be "older," not wiser. The rewards of settling down to live a life of domestic bliss dwarfed the benefits of his constant wanderings. Otherwise, Kerouac himself would become a ragged, flannel-shirted apparition, a forlorn ghost beneath looming finger-pointing clouds. He was himself the "Shrouded Traveler," a ragged spirit lost in America.

Furthermore, Gerard's estimation of Kerouac's friends and acquaintances was encouraging. He favored people like Ginsberg, Meyer Shapiro, and Alfred Kazin, who were "great men" for not trying to "dejew" themselves. Therefore, he advised that Kerouac should not "defrench" himself (advice he took to heart when he retained his small-town provincialism and "Frenchness" for interviews related to *On the Road*'s publication and for the rest of his career), but rather should write in French and attend masses. Not that he didn't already feel *different,* like those Jewish immigrants, or the Greeks, blacks,

Italians, and others who first stepped into the New World, clutching their paltry belongings, prayers and hopes.

Through some deft maneuvering using his friends as foils, Kerouac was able to convince the publicity department of Harcourt, Brace to give him money for a plane ticket to Denver, to attend an autographing session. Frugally, he used the funds for a bus ticket, stashing the rest for Denver.

After the bookstore signing in Denver, the prospect of going to Mexico became a real possibility. When William Burroughs received his personally inscribed copy of *The Town and the City,* he wrote to Kerouac, asking when he could make it down to Mexico. Burroughs's first real writing was underway, ultimately resulting in the novel *Junky,* later to be published in 1953 as a "two-in-one" thirty-five-cent Ace paperback original (credited to the pseudonymous William Lee). Burroughs was proud of his latest legal maneuvering of relocating out of the United States. He began filing papers for Mexican citizenship: "What a relief to be rid of the U.S. for good and all." In Mexico, after filing and receiving his pistol permit, Burroughs could now walk the streets protected with a holstered gun.

Good-byes for Kerouac were so difficult that he dreaded the night before his actual journey. To him, it was like the "night before death." Questioning his motives once again, he asked himself, "Where am I really going and what for?" "Why," he continued, "must I always travel from here to there, as if it mattered where one is?" His mother, slowly ironing his clothes and packing his bag, looked at her wayward son with a "furtive sadness." He said his good-bye to Cassady, who was in dirty overalls (and was barely getting by financially so that he was reduced to cheating his clients out of change), on the Madison Avenue parking lot. Carrying his bag that contained his road manuscript, he boarded his bus.

DENVER AGAIN

In Denver, considering the fate of *The Town and the City,* Kerouac's mood darkened considerably. His years of hard work had been casually dismissed in one deft put-down by a "know-nothing" critic. On the other hand, his Denver buddies Ed White and Frank Jeffries rejoiced in his newfound celebrity, making him feel both at home and important. Even Bob Burford's sister Beverly attached herself to Kerouac, sensing the nurturing he needed. Women were sometimes only too glad to accommodate Kerouac with his movie-star looks. However, pervasive gloom seemed to follow him like thunderclouds as he drank, watched, and listened. More than likely he was thinking of *On the Road.* He now thought of titling it *Gone on the Road,* and how it would more fully define him as a serious novelist than *The Town and the City* had failed to do.

At the thinly attended book-signing, a flannel-suited Kerouac sat with Justin Brierly and looked at the piles of books, realizing that four years of his life were contained between the two hard covers. However, his gloom lifted when Neal

Cassady burst suddenly through the door, flashing a wide grin. Oily jeans and a torn T-shirt did little to impress the respectable Brierly, who frowned considerably at Cassady's antics, which only succeeded in lifting Kerouac's spirits.

Cassady was again on the run. This time it wasn't from Carolyn, who was initiating divorce proceedings, but from Diana Hansen, who was about to give birth. To legitimize the child, Cassady urgently needed to drive to Mexico and hasten the divorce proceedings so that he could marry Hansen. Looming large among his motives was a chance to get away from his low-paying job and see Kerouac, Mexico, and score some cheap, potent marijuana.

Cassady's inappropriate behavior clashed with the bookstore audience, who were under the impression that they were a part of some exclusive social sect and not a page from Kerouac's novel. The two old friends, who had already smoked a few bombs on their way from the notorious Elitch Gardens, stupidly grinned their way through the intellectual smugness. Cassady lusted after Al Hinkle's sister and tried to woo her, but she, like Helen Hinkle, called him the "devil incarnate."

Kerouac's rowdiness during the "Neal" phase of his Denver trip was noticeable to some. The dark mood that had threatened to totally isolate Kerouac dissipated; he had taken to smoking pot and drinking more than usual. Punching walls in a bathroom with Neal was a stark contrast to lounging in a chair, chin down to his chest, eyes closed, absorbing the sounds and conversations around him. At the Windsor Hotel, Cassady harmed his other thumb by repeatedly punching the men's room door. He had reason for his stoned rage: this was the same hotel he had lived in with his drunk father as a child and its memories stirred intense dislike. The damage would swell his knuckle to an alarming size months after the incident.

Cassady let his friend Frank Jeffries accompany Kerouac and himself to Mexico. Jeffries's free-spirit appealed to Cassady, guaranteeing stimulating company. Loaded up with luggage, food, and water, the car fled Denver toward the dark southern plains. Kerouac, through the rear window, watched the Mile High City fade into the distance, the land bruised purple before darkening completely and vanishing.

The '36 Chevy plumed dust through New Mexico and into Texas, where Cassady planned on crossing the border. After Fredericksburg, Abilene, and San Antonio, the air turned arid, baking the land around them like a brick oven. In that city, they stopped to "goof," noting that San Antonio resembled Mexico more than Texas. In a pool hall, they dug a crippled boy trying his best to bank shots and win some money from people who, they intuited, had made him the "butt of jokes." Then Kerouac imagined he could smell the Rio Grande's ruffled waters coasting on their way to the Gulf of Mexico. When they reached the South Texas Crossroads, a region of Texas that hosts three major intersecting highways, they decided to put in at Victoria and visit a whorehouse. (Victoria was to be one of the film locations for the 1982 film version of *The Best Little Whorehouse in Texas*.) They left and turned the car west for Laredo, the Rio Grande, and finally, Mexico.

Howling with delight, they exchanged their United States currency at the rate of eight Mexican pesos for each dollar. Their fat bankrolls encouraged them to indulge freely in drinking, eating, and the numerous Mexican prostitutes milling around the market districts. After a full appreciation of the tawny, shapely women with long black hair, they moved on toward Monterrey. At the higher altitude, the air began to cool. They could see the snow-capped peaks of the Sierra Madre. Though Kerouac wanted to stop and take in the city of the clouds, Cassady urged them to keep going, for he imagined more interesting sights were in store for them in Mexico City.

Montemorelos, in the Mexican state of Nuevo León, bordered the Rio Pilón, its chief crop being oranges. As the car descended, the air again grew denser, hot, and seemingly more virile. A distinct air of Catholicism hung like verdant clouds over the city. Men walked carrying machetes along the dirt roads, and the homes were nothing more than thatched huts deep in the bush. Kerouac took the wheel through Linares and then the game-rich but steamy city of Rio Soto la Marina. He noted that he was, at last, among the Fellaheen. In *On the Road,* he explains at length:

> Fellahin Indians of the world, the essential strain of the basic primitive, wailing humanity that stretches in a belt around the equatorial belly of the world from Malaya (the long fingernail of China) to India the great subcontinent to Arabia to Morocco to the selfsame deserts and jungles of Mexico and over the waves to Polynesia to mystic Siam of the Yellow Robe and on around, on around, so that you hear the same mournful wail by the rotted walls of Cadiz, Spain, that you hear 12,000 miles around in the depths of Benares the Capital of the World.

The dark countenance of the natives he saw indicated that they ascended from ancient strains, not from Spanish invaders who had decimated those who had thrived here for thousands of years. Their cheekbones were more defined, eyes clear and serene, giving them a gaunt, holy expression of inner resolve.

In Gregoria, Kerouac solicited from a young boy information leading to a prostitute for Cassady, as he'd promised him in San Antonio. Later, the boy supplied them with freshly dried pot and rolled a joint the size of a cigar (using a brown paper bag as his rolling paper). The high was tremendous, an amazing "billowy trip in the world" (the name of an excerpt from *On the Road* published in *New Directions 16* two months before the publication of the novel in September 1957). Later, the boy took them to a whorehouse. Mexican police officers stood indifferently at the doors of the establishment, glancing at the three men with slight interest. Inside, a jukebox blared songs, while women, dark-lidded and mysterious, appeared as if they had escaped from western films. They danced with the girls, eyeing even those young ones who would have otherwise landed them in jail in the United States.

The next day, they left. The road plunged into a chaos of towering trees after crossing the Tropic of Cancer north of Mazatlan. It was nighttime in El Limón and Cassady vowed to sleep in the jungle, an unwise aspiration given the swampy heat and the swarming insects out to quench their thirst for blood. Kerouac, who despised extreme heat in the first place (and would later scorn Florida for that very same reason), tried to get comfortable in the car, to no avail. He watched the night policeman make his rounds in the village before tottering closer to the car. He made a polite inquiry about their intentions before moving on. Unlike the police back home, who made life difficult for hoboes and transients, there were no complications with the law. Burroughs, Kerouac thought, was absolutely right.

Long stretches driving through the jungle, where the people seemed alien, pushed them onward, zealous to absorb every detail about this great and ancient land. Before long they reached the Sierra Madre Oriental, a region with immense pine-oak forests. On the other side was the last long leg of the journey to Mexico City. Here the natives were dressed in desert shawls and carried immense bundles of flax, one of their chief means of commerce and sustenance.

All at once, Mexico City, all 572 square miles nestled inside a volcanic range, lay before them. Kerouac could see industrial smoke rising, a harbinger of the pollution that later choked the city deep within its volcanic crater. He, Cassady, and Jeffries wound their way through the congested city streets looking for Burroughs's place at Cerrada Meddelin. Kerouac observed that Mexico City bore an eerie resemblance to Lowell; it shared the same Catholic overtones, the same provincialism, and people who shuffled along the sidewalks the same way as those old women shopping along Lowell's Merrimack Street. It was, he realized, a universal resemblance that never changed, no matter where he stood in the wide world.

SMART WENT CRAZY

William Burroughs's reasons for favoring Mexico were altogether different. He believed in living out a life, no matter how hedonistic and vilified it might be, without intrusion by the law. Here, the law was reduced to passive civil servants. Any scofflaw among these relatively gentle people was handled within the social circle where it arose. Burroughs found that carrying a .45 magnum in his holster avoided any trouble and that the only thing the Mexican authorities seemed to frown upon specifically was the extensive drug trafficking that infiltrated the underground economy. Even this was subject to a payoff if and when one found the right person.

Burroughs's court case in New Orleans was an impending storm waiting to burst. Drug possession in the States was a serious crime that, before the wrong judge, could hold grave consequences. The Colinal Roma section of Mexico, where he chose to live, was a viper's nest of vice, just the thing to appeal to Burroughs's criminal sensibility. Gay hustler bars prospered next to meat markets, and gambling houses regularly held cockfights, which Burroughs enjoyed for their "brutal, bloody, and degrading" spectacle. Prostitutes, alarming numbers of them, were there for the taking and seemed to Kerouac mysterious and threatening, descriptions he would use for prostitutes hiding in the shadowy doorways of Tangier years later. (Mexico was, Burroughs wrote Kerouac, an "Oriental country that reflects 2,000 years of disease and poverty and degradation and stupidity and slavery and brutality and psychic and physical terrorism.") Furthermore, he warned Kerouac, Mexico was "sinister and gloomy and chaotic with the special chaos of a dream." All this subverted the Fellaheen idealization Kerouac foisted upon these discouraged and struggling people.

With his monthly allowance of $200, Burroughs found he could reasonably prosper even though his morphine habit sometimes cost him thirty dollars at a take. A new acquaintance, the diminutive drug addict "Old Dave" Tesorero and his junky girlfriend, Esperanza Villanueva (who Kerouac later used as the subject of his novella *Tristessa*) made his living, for the while, selling cheap faux silver crucifixes to legions of worshipers. Burroughs and Tesorero schemed of the latter's taking advantage of the legal government rations for drug addicts (15 grams monthly at a cost of two dollars per gram), with Burroughs paying for half. This transaction assured a constant high throughout the month.

Kerouac's experience in Mexico City was also a perpetual high that assured him a blissful, if discombobulated, look at the life he revered so much. He told John Clellon Holmes that he planned to smoke "increasingly larger bombers until finally I will know "the end of the night." The experience, though it seems to have inspired him in a hallucinatory way, hurt the progress of his road novel, for his days were spent, like Burroughs's, sitting in a stoned stupor watching the fellaheen world pass him by.

Returning home one Sunday afternoon after visiting a bullfight, Kerouac decided that he had to pay penance for the death of the bull. He was disgusted and sick at heart at the bloody spectacle of a sixteen-inch sword stabbed so deep into the side of the bull that it pierced its heart and caused "rivers of blood" to spew forth. As the tormented creature tossed its head, blood foamed from its mouth until it collapsed, bellowing its last desperate breath. Afterward, horses dragged the bull away and men, armed with shovels, scooped up coagulating blood and sprinkled sand over the crimson stains. Kerouac left and walked across the desert until he approached an ancient Indian village along the dribble of a brown stream. It was a housing development. Close by, etched in sharp relief against the sinking sun, was a pile of orange bricks. Higher than he had ever been before, he imagined God waiting for him at this makeshift altar to "have a word with me." As the heat seeped into his body, he sat and feasted upon a "swirl" of hallucinatory images. One was the Great Walking Saint who, like Kerouac, was doomed to walk across the great wild expanse of America until the day he died. In the process, the spector would "dig all things; men and women, animals, trees, flowers and the many rivers that intersected, criss-crossing the continent like arterial passages engorging the earth with life."

It was the capstone to the road novel; it was Kerouac himself, doing his penance, walking for the bull across the heated earth. The Saint sits on a rock speaking to children listening to the "hum of time." His elongated shadow stretched across Highway 66 asking drivers, destined nowhere, "Whither goest thou?" The Great Walking Saint, an enigmatic figure sitting in the middle of Mexican shacks, spoke to the natives in his strange tongue, and doubtless, thought Kerouac, they understood him. And he walks on and on, at the age of seventy, even at one hundred. Kerouac would do so, too, like Leo Tolstoy, who gave up his affluent lifestyle and took to the Russian roads seeking redemption and communion with God.

Kerouac, as he told John Clellon Holmes, had seen the

"light," and, furthermore, the "end of the night" perching upon that precipice that made all things possible. Resigning his "optimism," he was completely convinced that the world he lived in was one of bloodshed, mindless violence and he, as witness, felt like a "Jew" scratching his name inside a concentration camp cell sealed to his fate and accepting the inevitable doom that comes to us all.

Kerouac came down with dysentery; fevered and drained from frequent diarrhea, he was down and out when Cassady came to his bedside and told him he was leaving. He had obtained the divorce papers he needed so that he could marry Diana. He left Kerouac and Jeffries to their own devices to get home safely. About a week after the bullfighting incident and his vision of the Great Walking Saint, Kerouac left, too.

With a kilo of cured marijuana safely concealed in a silk scarf he tied around his waist, he boarded the Ferrocarril de Mexico Pullman car that took him all the way to Laredo, Texas. In San Antonio, he boarded a bus with a stopover in Baltimore, Maryland. Then New York. He looked forward to his writing desk in Richmond Hill and to once again considering the vastness of Manhattan with all of its possibilities.

EYEBALL KICKS

At the end of July, Kerouac received a new letter from Neal Cassady that spilled out the details of his solo flight from

Mexico in his broken-down car. He had driven through the great mountain passes, back through the swampy heat where once again he slept naked, bitten by clouds of bloodthirsty insects. In Victoria, he bought a stash of pot that was so powerful that it threw him into a hallucinatory fever; it was the "greatest shit the world has ever known." Driving the car without distraction, he experienced "eyeball kicks." "I became so engrossed in my eyeballs & what they brought me over each ridge & thru each town that I looked out into the world as one looks into a picture." His visionary field became his personal canvas where he could slip off whenever he felt the slightest ennui.

However, the car was in a sorry state. In Linares, he changed the fan belt and repaired the carburetor, at the cost of a twelve-hour delay and an exorbitant fee. After driving a police chief and a sheriff's deputy from Linares to Monterrey, he realized the car's generator was in disrepair and he had to drive the 150 miles without headlights to North Laredo. If he turned off the ignition switch, he knew the car would never start again.

After successfully passing through United States customs with his pot safely concealed, he had the car's generator repaired and went on to Houston. The following morning, he experienced more problems. In Lake Charles, Louisiana, an experienced mechanic discovered that the rear end of the car had separated from the axle. In desperation, Cassady sold the car for $32 and flew the remainder of the trip to New York on a four-engine Constellation.

At home, high on his Mexican tea, he hassled with Diana about their questionable future together. In a letter to Kerouac, he failed to mention that he had married Diana on July 10, 1950, with Allen Ginsberg, John Clellon Holmes, and Alan Harrington as witnesses. Four hours after the last-minute ceremony officiated by a priest, Cassady was gone to San Francisco, having secured work with the Southern Pacific Railroad, leaving Diana to honeymoon alone.

In San Francisco, after Carolyn refused to let him sleep in a bed in her Russell Street house, he rented a room in a shabby hotel. He wrote Diana, imploring her to come out west to live. Having each other, after all, was better than having nobody. If she chose to stay in New York, he would live with her for six months during the winter when there was no railroad work, and return to San Francisco (to stay with Carolyn) for the remainder of the year. If she did choose to come, she could live at the opposite end of the long train tracks and, advantageously, Cassady could coast back and forth by rail to see either her or Carolyn at a moment's notice. Neither plan gelled, leaving him with the only option he always relied upon, impulsion and flight whenever he was backed into a corner by domestication and responsibility.

The actual marriage papers brought back from Mexico City, "twenty sheets of foolscap" festooned with waxen red seals turned out to be invalid, thus falsifying the marriage into a bigamous union. Diana had assumed that he had already informed Carolyn of his intentions, particularly after her pregnancy. His insistence on the Mexico trip and the speed of his divorce suggests that he did not want this child to be born out of wedlock. It was also possible that Cassady truly wanted to settle down, as Kerouac had a month before.

Carolyn, however, did not wish to start anew with Cassady, having taken, under duress, her first steps toward independence. She did consent to let him spend time with his neglected children at her apartment. He had successfully arranged Diana's visit to an apartment he rented in Watsonville but, not long after she arrived, she visited Carolyn against Carolyn's wishes. Cassady dropped in, oblivious that the two were together—and no doubt discussing his irresponsibility. He argued with Diana while Carolyn heatedly ridiculed him. He spent the remainder of his stay in Watsonville, once summoning LuAnne for a visit. They, too, argued and Cassady left the apartment, moving back to San Francisco in the Haight-Ashbury district.

RICHMOND HILL

Kerouac's life in Richmond Hill with his mother was far less complicated than Cassady's was. Though content to be writing once again at his beloved desk with his mother fawning over him, he still craved a wife, misguidedly believing that having one meant maternal solicitude with the added bonus of sexual pleasure. He craved simplicity in his life. Even this, however, became increasingly difficult.

The cold war and the Red Scare, for all of their prominence in the nation, did not seem to affect Kerouac or what he was attempting to write at the time, at least overtly. His personal utopia of drugs and sexual hedonism as a means to universal consciousness was all he was concerned with. Even when President Truman committed American arms to defend South Korea from communist North Korea, Kerouac's response was to stand by the spiritual guidance of guardian angels, for the mounting casualties of American troops meant it was "time to say good-bye all around" (Jack Kerouac to Jim Sampas, August 1, 1950).

Slowly, he began altering the style of his writing to reflect his recent metaphysical experiences. The copious writing from Neal Cassady helped stimulate Kerouac's creative juices, especially since he had purchased a tape recorder. Kerouac once recorded himself with Cassady during one of their stoned rap sessions and transcribed it faithfully for the experimental novel *Visions of Cody.* Cassady saw the possibility of it also; such a device could save him the hassle of writing long letters. Instead, he could unwind a "5,000 page" letter every day. Experimenting, Cassady bought a copy of Thomas Wolfe's *Of Time and the River* and read pages of it into the microphone. He did the same with Marcel Proust's *Remembrance of Things Past.*

More importantly, for Kerouac, Cassady's letters of the fall of 1950 pointed the way to another writing breakthrough for him. High on pot, Cassady dispensed with mechanics and emphasized feeling over craft. He was now with Carolyn, writing his book under her approving eyes, glad to see him focused on *something* constructive. Kerouac's letters to him were also of great importance, assuring him that he was not alone in his "mental world," and that the two of them shared an affinity for pure abstraction in their storytelling. Dwelling on details and sexual frankness oftentimes pointed the way to complete and honest liberation of the word. Depressed by his everyday surroundings, Cassady retreated into a creative netherworld.

To Kerouac, he described his writing as dropping into the "deepest parts of the mind until they are sunlit corners because one recognizes them so well because of the repetition and emotional strength of the deeper images." He felt it was best to vent in abstraction rather than letting the torments of his thoughts grow stale in the void of his heart and soul: "any thought, no matter how gone becomes so binded and cramped that the vegetation entangles itself endlessly and rots in jungle fashion of rot." It was an aesthetic that was both overwhelming in its intensity and sheer volume, so much so that he could not keep up with his racing thoughts until the "whole fuckin shop closes on wildcat strike."

Cassady was buoyed now by Carolyn's acceptance of him back into her life. When he wasn't tending to his numerous injuries and ailments at the Southern Pacific Hospital, he wrote to Diana. Crassly, he informed her that he spent what little else he had "fucking" his still-legitimate wife. Even this began to stale for him, and he planned on leaving once again. He was anxious to take to the road, and perhaps make the trip to Mexico an annual one. He was now "Keroassady," and, being so, expected to get back to New York in as little as ten weeks. His intention was to arrive with a new car, take Kerouac back to Mexico with him, and begin where they left off. Kerouac, however, had other plans.

CHANGES

The aborted *Gone on the Road* (begun on July 26, 1950, in Richmond Hill) begins with a chapter entitled "An Awkward Man." The "awkwardness" of the first-person narrator is due to a temporary loss of identity. This feeling occurs when the narrator awakes in an old beat hotel room with the shades drawn. He has no idea if it is day or night, and "in the space of five or six seconds [. . .] I completely lost every faintest, poorest, most woeful recollection of who I was." The work struggled for a few more pages until Kerouac gave it up completely. The bulk of the work was basically a sounding board for his self-defeating attitude toward himself: "I stared in the mirror to see the damage of the slob, grieving, all-grieving at the sight of it, astonished at the suffering face I saw, horrified by the drawn, hooded eye that looked at me." Kerouac gave this version of *On the Road* to Bob Giroux for his consideration, who flatly rejected it. Farrar, Straus asked for further revisions before they would consider the book at all. When he attempted to do so, he felt that he was better off just rewriting the whole thing from scratch.

One of the more important discoveries he had made during October 1950 was the importance of voice in writing. Listening to the World Series on the radio, he noticed that the sports announcers captured the thrill of the game with their clever use of adjectives. Such was his fascination of capturing distinct American vernacular and colloquialisms that he envisioned writing an American Times Series. This work would capture the narrations of the "voices of Americans themselves," including a first part narrated by a ten-year-old African American boy (published posthumously as *Pic,* a novella, in 1971). Other voices he wanted to capture were Mexicans, French Canadians, Westerners, Italians, jail-birds, hipsters, and hoboes. More than any of them, he focused on distilling the pure locus of Neal Cassady, rendering all of his mortal trappings onto the written page.

Kerouac urged Cassady to keep writing the way he did. He was so taken with Cassady's stoned spiel of sensory language that he was tempted to type it up verbatim, to experience the direct application of confessional writing himself. In response to a letter from Cassady, he told him on October 6, 1950, "It was the best letter I ever received and the best letter you ever wrote in your life." He thought that Cassady, for once, had not hung himself up on maintaining a "literary" voice. He had captured the magic that Shakespeare experienced with Hamlet—when Hamlet spoke, it sounded like Hamlet's voice, not

Shakespeare's. Wild, ebullient, frank, and honest, moving with the discordant complexities of bop jazz, using the voice and spirit of Neal Cassady as his guiding stick, Kerouac at last was on to something that would make a stylistic difference. It was, in his estimation, the "long confession of two buddies telling everything that ever happened, every detail, every cunt-hair in the grass, every tiny eyeball flick of orange neon flashed past in Chicago in the bus station; all the back of the brain imagery." Another aspect of his writing, most evident from a letter of November 5, 1950, was Cassady's graphic sexuality. The word "cunt" was pervasive, often linked to a string of adjectives connected to it ("juicy & ripe"). Descriptions of sexual acts prevail: "In fact, pal, if you love me, you'll do all in your power to find a girl, any girl (like em skinny) (for fuckin' that is, you see, skinny girls are all CUNT) & tell her I can fuck all night & blow them till their belly falls out & get their cunt inside out so I can fuck them to the real bottom, not that I can't anyhow, with a little cooperation." "Cunt" is also used pejoratively: "but get a cunt & your cunt & us'll have a *real* orgy unless you want to go lonely fucker." Though Kerouac was initially prudish about embellishing his own sexual experience (except to Neal), he later surrendered his reticence and incorporated graphic sexual passages into *Visions of Cody,* thus making it impossible for squeamish publishers to ever print it in Kerouac's lifetime (with the exception of "safe" excerpts). Kerouac's admittance that the discovery of his mature writing style came only after "reading the marvelous free narrative letters of Neal Cassady" indicates a fairly accurate barometer shift in Kerouac's prose; a melange of graphic street talk and highly original poetry.

MARRIAGE

Twenty-year-old Joan Haverty was raised in Poughkeepsie, New York. When she met Jack, she was living in New York City with Bill Cannastra, a man who met his fate in the dark subway tunnels of Manhattan after he attempted to climb out of the moving window of the subway car. His skull was crushed against a granite support pillar. Ten days after Cannastra's untimely death, Kerouac and Haverty decided to marry, on November 17, 1950.

Joan had planned on having only a few invited guests for the wedding, but two hundred turned out for the rooftop festivities. Joan already felt detached from Kerouac's crowd and, by the time the night was over, she was faced with a floor littered with cigarette butts, an overflowing beer keg, a clogged toilet, and a rotting mass of Vienna sausages that had fallen behind the refrigerator. Their first night together as husband and wife came to nil after the groom passed out on the bed, but the next day Kerouac suspected he had conceived a child.

Writing to Allen Ginsberg in November, Cassady described his newest saga of misfortune: he felt harried by Kerouac and Diana (for whom he was to obtain railroad passes), veterinary care for his daughter's cocker spaniel, his own lack of medical care, tending to the overgrown backyard for his daughter to play in, and an inability to complete even the most mundane and simple tasks (including changing spark plugs, brushing his teeth, and even sleeping). His mind was frazzled from too much pot (though he was asking Ginsberg to send him more via the U.S. mail), not enough sleep, and his own pathology that threatened to engulf him completely. Cassady also felt that the pot he and Kerouac smoked in Mexico was so potent that it made him lose himself in thoughts he may never otherwise have had. Cassady fought incessantly with abstractions: "Easier to break up a theme of Beethoven with a knife than break up the soul by methods of abstract thought" (Cassady to Allen Ginsberg, November 25, 1950). He and Carolyn began reading Oswald Spengler, so instead of opening him up, the pot and literature made him more instrospective.

Ginsberg broke the news of Kerouac's marriage to Cassady. For all of his confusion and torment, Cassady commented to Ginsberg that he felt Kerouac's brooding in Richmond Hill was a "final and most disheartening realization of himself." Though he did not feel that Kerouac was unhappy, "it was that itself which showed him the truth of the matter." Kerouac's constant "blasting" of marijuana in Mexico left him almost completely out of it for "long periods of time." Being so stoned, Cassady determined, only made one feel how absolutely alone one was, how unable to make oneself "clear" to others. The "difficulties of yourself tracing the trail of inner feeling and conviction are so insurmountable that not only in writing, but even speech and action, one is completely misunderstood." The distortions of what one was trying to express made people see only the "caricature" of what one was attempting to say, rather than the actual kernel of thought originally conceived.

Furthermore, Neal Cassady sincerely felt that had Kerouac not been so stoned all of the time, he wouldn't be married. It was, Cassady felt (for he was married three times to attest to this fact), an act of "willful blindness." Kerouac would only cater to Joan's "shallowness" in order to have her "bodys fullness." He was unable to meet anybody's personal demands, especially a female's, so therefore his was a marriage doomed to fail. If it was to last at all, it would only be from her capacity to leave "Jack alone." For now, Joan Haverty was the "girl with the pure and innocent deer eyes that [he] had always searched for and for so long."

Kerouac was excited by the prospect of his new marriage. With joyous optimism, he informed Cassady that Joan seemed positive about going to Mexico City and living there with him. During the honeymoon, Kerouac convinced Joan to move out of her old apartment, where the signs of the dead man who used to occupy it were displayed in a makeshift shrine she had created. They went to his mother's apartment at Richmond Hill in order to save money for their trip to Mexico. In Mexico, he thought, they would live so cheaply that he could write as much as he liked and still support a wife.

While Gabrielle watched the news about the heightened

tensions of the Korean War (only five days before, the Chinese had sent two million soldiers to attack allied troops in Korea), and Joan showering, Kerouac rolled a joint and wrote to Cassady. Of late he had been sharing Cassady's letters with his wife as a sort of introduction to his friend and the world of the road he inhabited when he wasn't home. In addition to the Mexico trip, he informed Cassady that he was putting aside his road novel, to make money synopsizing scripts for Twentieth-Century Fox. This temporary aside, a desperate attempt to be a breadwinner, only put the novel on the back burner. He fumbled once again with what to call the work-in-progress so that it would truly capture the spirit of the novel: "Down the Road Night," "American Road Night," "Look Out for Your Boy," "Boy on the Road," "Hit the Road," "Lost on the Road," "Souls on the Road," "Love on the Road," "In the Night on the Road," "Home on the Road," and "Along the Wild Road."

One of his plans to maintain a semblance of domestic bliss was to move himself and Joan to San Francisco and secure a job as a sports reporter for the *San Francisco Chronicle*. These were valiant stabs at keeping his marriage intact, for Kerouac was proud of Joan's beauty and intelligence. Boastingly, he sent Cassady her photograph, describing her as the youthful Gloria Jean from the 1941 film *Never Give a Sucker an Even Break*.

Meanwhile, Kerouac remained sullen about the failure of *The Town and the City* to win book-reading audiences. Kerouac opined that the fate of his book was the work of critics who couldn't think for themselves, dooming serious and challenging works of fiction to extinction. (He had a point. By this time most of William Faulkner's novels were out of print. Only after receiving the Nobel Peace Prize in 1949 did his reputation as a novelist begin to recover). He was also bitter over a bar fight in which he had defended a bilious Lucien Carr against a soldier who had thrown beer in his face. One of the soldier's friends punched Kerouac in the eye and kneed his testicles. It was an unfortunate distraction from the more positive, constructive path he was on, one that took a decisive turn after he received Cassady's written response on December 17–22, 1950. On the top of the letter Cassady wrote "PERSONAL: For Security Reasons." Enclosed was a runaway train of rambling prose exorcizing his past.

THE "JOAN ANDERSON" LETTER

"To have seen a specter isn't everything, and there are death-masks piled, one atop the other, clear to heaven." The type-written letter, a fireworks display of ebullient verbosity and grotesqueries, appealed significantly to Kerouac, for it was surely written with his keen eye in mind. He, like Cassady, had "lifted the veil" of mortality mentioned in the body of the letter.

The surviving portion of the letter opens with Cassady and an unnamed woman, presumably a girlfriend who has just had an abortion. As she lies on a hospital bed, Cassady's description of her is one of controlled bleakness: her skin is stark white, in contrast to her jet-black matted hair; her face glooms as a chalky "death mask," her soft cadaverous eyes closed until Cassady looms over her. They open before making hesitant contact. Later on, when Joan is in a bathroom alone with Cassady, she opens her bathrobe to reveal a scar stretching from her navel to her vagina. Neal's impulse is to leave her suddenly, get a clean set of clothes, and take a cab-driving job offered by her friends. The letter is full of outrageous escapades and an almost slapstick brand of black humor, culminating in Cassady's escape through the bathroom window after dallying with a piece of jailbait nicknamed Cherry Mary. His dark world of birth and abortion, bleak descriptions and frank sexuality, though not directly catering to Kerouac's taste, certainly appealed to him in a frank, confessional way.

The writing was part of an autobiographical piece of prose Cassady was randomly typing in his attic space (later published as *The First Third*). Though minimal in page count, this work became vastly important to Jack Kerouac and Allen Ginsberg, who knew and understood where their friend was coming from: destitution, hobo alleys, broken whiskey bottles, bleak hung-over mornings, seedy street hustlers and panhandlers, sexual predation, car thefts during the Great Depression, an era when most could not get ahead except through street smarts and preying on those who did not know any better. It was the portrait of an "urban cowboy," as Lawrence Ferlinghetti describes it in the editor's note in *The First Third*.

The writing was also a direct mimicry of Cassady's speech

and ancestry. He set about mythologizing his own life. His prologue hearkens back to the days of Cassady's grandfathers, from his forefather's first arrival in America to his father losing his barbershop due to "nonsobriety" and general ineptness. It is a sincere effort on Neal's part to take a serious pitch at writing. Although the prologue is carefully written with extensive revision, the remainder of his prose becomes more and more reckless as he learns, at a much faster rate than Kerouac, to dispense with grammar, mechanics, and sentence structure in favor of capturing anxiety, guilt and embellished recollection. Though Kerouac may have read these pieces and was impressed by them, he was inspired the most from Cassady's letters. Neal Cassady was writing through his correspondence of his own bleak life, having nothing to lose by telling the truth.

When the lengthy letter arrived, Kerouac picked it up from the front steps and proceeded to read it not once but three times in full on the same day. That evening, he shared it with Joan, who was so caught up in the story that dinner was delayed for an hour. Kerouac responded immediately, with generous comparisons to Dostoevsky, opining that he ranked the letter "among the best things ever written in America." The confessional weave of the narrative fully justified its exposition; each part told a story cinematically. Kerouac showed the letter to John Clellon Holmes and Alan Harrington, but neither was impressed by what they read. Cassady had written the letter with great "rapidity"; it was through its speedy narrative that the thrust of the prose lay intact like a slumbering tiger. These "poolhall musings" achieved what Kerouac had sought to accomplish in his own writing years earlier. Inspired, Kerouac sat down at his desk the evening of December 28, 1950, and began to write his own autobiographical tome. "The time has come for me to write a full confession of my life to you." And that he did.

CONFESSION

The act of doing this wasn't merely an act of generosity on Kerouac's behalf, it was his attempt to "renounce all fiction." "Neal, this confession is for YOU, and through you to God, and through God back to my life, and wife, whatever and what-all." Over the course of five letters, he generated his earliest childhood memories, both remembered and imagined: his birth at March's first thaw; the strangeness of its attending "red afternoon light"; the sickly Gerard; the dying Gerard; the parochial school with pedophile priests at basement urinals; a dying mouse Gerard saves from a mousetrap (all of which was exploited for great effect in *Visions of Gerard,* 1963); and of Gerard's scolding of the world for inflicting suffering upon all living things.

One senses Kerouac was in a trance, totally engrossed in his interior memories, shadowy recollections of his past, some starkly recalled, others vividly imagined. He continued, seeing the past now like a stream of liquid fire, as stark and instant as a Polaroid snapshot: Gerard watching "heaven" as he lay in the backyard grass; the haunting of bedrooms—an ominous foreboding silent film from Lowell's Rialto Theatre he saw as a boy—crisscrossed with flashing lights on his bedroom ceiling, plaster crumbling; a tall, Nosferatu-like figure looming over his crib; Gerard slapping his face after Kerouac knocked over an Erector set construction, an act as trivial as it was impulsive, yet one that stamped Kerouac with indelible guilt; his brother's untimely death, in the springtime, the season of his own birth; the guilt Kerouac harbored at wishing his brother's death after the slap and that it had come true. Rain, horse-drawn hearses, little boys acting as coffin bearers, the rain-swept funeral, the little wooden box splatted with springtime loam as rain pelted the coffin lid embossed with a silver crucifix. An umarked plot, the boy for all intents and purposes forgotten save for the immediate family that would never forget and, in some ways, now split into a jigsaw puzzle of abstract dysfunction. Afterward, Kerouac saw and felt the unimaginable grief of his mother, the wet tears of morning and the same at night, moving to a house neighbored by a graveyard and stark bare trees bordering its iron gates. Gabrielle losing all of her teeth, symptomatic of extreme grief, hugging the one she had that much closer so that literally and figuratively she would never let go for the rest of his life.

The second letter continues after Gerard's death, when Kerouac's reveries of what he actually remembered become crystal clear. He suffers a sensory overload of imagined ghosts haunting his house on Hildreth Street and slowly realizes that memories are indeed inseparable from dreams. Also conjured up from this sensory wellspring is the castle of "Snake Hill," so named because of the garter snakes that made the Merrimack Valley its home (and later utilized for dramatic effect in *Doctor Sax*). The letter is also embellished with Catholic superstitions, notably the turning head of a marble statue of Saint Thérèse of Liseux.

The fourth and fifth letters continue in the same vein. On January 9, 1951, Kerouac completed the last of his five confessional letters, a vast undertaking of psychic mining committed to paper for his friend's eyes only (though later on, he and Cassady exchanged their lifetime of letters for safe archival keeping). He ended it simply, "Goodnight Sweet Prince."

Exhausted by his efforts, Kerouac's next string of letters to Cassady became more practical, as he had begun attempting to realize his plans to bring his wife to California.

Cassady had planned on arriving in New York City by February 1951. He was eager to meet his new son, Curtis, as well as somewhat anxious about seeing Jack and meeting his new bride. He wanted to return from New York to Denver to visit his father, who was now sentenced to the county jail in lieu of paying a $300 fine for some unspecified charge. Neal Sr. had pencilled a letter to his son wishing that he could see his new grandson. He also reminded his son of his own pride of fatherhood when he held Neal Jr. in his arms as a proud parent.

Kerouac responded excitedly that he was prepared to hire a panel truck (a windowless van built upon a truck chassis and usually used for food deliveries) per Cassady's advice. It would cost about ninety-five dollars to rent it cross-country. They could layer the floor with bookcases and put a mattress atop, allowing him and Joan to take turns sleeping during their nonstop cross-country trek to San Francisco. For extra funds, the pair planned on going to Washington, D.C., to extract money from Joan's father. Kerouac pleaded with Cassady to provide a vacant apartment on Russell Street in Russian Hill, not far from Cassady and Carolyn's. It was to be furnished in Bohemian sprawl; Jack foresaw a single mattress on the floor, candles, some bread and a jar of jam. They would build on that as a couple. Kerouac's hope to obtain a $1000 advance for *On the Road* was now unlikely, for he didn't yet have a polished manuscript to hand in.

Kerouac's flawed domestic idealism began to crumble. However genuine it was—for he was used to living on the barest necessities—it wasn't the vision his wife shared. Soon after their wedding, the first of their many troubles began to bubble up and Joan was already searching for a way out.

HOME WITH GABRIELLE

Gabrielle's imposing presence in the house had put a damper on Joan's efforts to reach out to her, or to win favoritism by helping out around the house. Joan felt like a teenager again, living with a stifling mother-figure who maintained her own way of doing things. Furthermore, Kerouac still clung to his mother, sometimes turning over to Gabrielle any thing Joan refused to do, even if she was tired from her department store job. If he wanted Joan to bake a cake and she demurred on principle, Gabrielle would undermine her by warming up the oven. Joan was obligated to hand over her paycheck and, again like a teenager, receive an allowance for the rest of the week. She was often shut out of many conversations because she did not understand French. She suspected that most times she was the subject of their conversation.

Also, Kerouac had a habit of sleeping in long after his wife had left for work. His constant brooding and self-absorption shut her out, sometimes so much that he hardly acknowledged her presence. Determined to salvage her life, Joan made plans to move into her own apartment. He was adamant that she couldn't leave, but he was backed into an awkward corner, having to choose between his wife or his mother.

Coming home from work one day, Joan saw that the moving truck she had hired was stalled by Kerouac's efforts to move his writing desk as well. After much convincing, the movers agreed with him, to Joan's disbelief. It was at this 454

West Twentieth Street apartment that he began typing the legendary scroll version of *On the Road*.

DEAN MORIARTY ON THE ROAD

William S. Burroughs began making preparations to leave Mexico for a time in order to travel to South America. He had been writing steadily and now was ready to show off his work to his writer friends. He mailed to Kerouac and Ginsberg the manuscript of *Junky* (titled *Junk* at that time). Kerouac was impressed with Burroughs's adaptation of Dashiell Hammett's writing style and its straightforward prose. Burroughs effectively avoided the temptation to insert flowery prose or any other mode of expression that wasn't his true voice. It was Burroughs's voice throughout and Kerouac could almost hear his sardonic drone and black wit shining through the pages of the manuscript like poisoned diamonds.

Burroughs wasn't the only one working on a novel. John Clellon Holmes was still writing *Go,* a novel peopled with his New York friends and acquaintances. In March 1950, Holmes approached Kerouac with his completed manuscript, to solicit some critical advice. Holmes found that relying on autobiography was not enough; he needed imagination to flesh out the novel. Though Kerouac initially praised Holmes's work, he later felt Holmes had imitated his own style (as well as the subject matter) after the novel was published to good reviews in the fall of 1952.

Before Cassady left for the West Coast, he wrote Kerouac another letter. He was not leaving on January 3; the promised railroad work again did not pan out. Instead, he had to take work in Oakland and plan on leaving by the end of the month. Again, his letter contained an impressive display of verbose wordplay, which became a hallmark of Kerouac's own mature writing:

> from the most ungentlemanly wound I create you shall suffer the stings of maddened wasps, your lifeblood shall flow unchecked, impotent rage will clutch your guts, joy will lose its bloom, saturated with despair you will fall to the floor cursing your fate, unrelished your love, unaware your mind, unsatisfied your sense, uncaring your eyes, unfulfilled your ambitions, unhinged your brain, unappreciated your talents, unlamented your future, unknown your life, understandable (that's a goodie) your underwear, unbuttoned your shoes (you vulgar square), untied your necktie, uncombed your hair, unzipped your fly (you vulgar modern), unapplied you're applepolish, deadpolish, toothpolish, bootpolish, fingernailpolishhamburger, unexcelled you're anguish, unparalleled your weeping, wailing, wallowing, groaning, griping . . ." (Neal Cassady to Jack Kerouac, December 30, 1950)

Cassady had promised to bring his tape recorder to New York and show Kerouac how he had been taping himself reading and playing the saxophone into it. However, he did not, and had no excuse to offer other than its weight (over fifty pounds) and bulkiness. The machine was also sensitive to temperature as well as somewhat fragile. Kerouac, eager to try some experiments of his own using the sounds of actual voices, would have to wait until arriving in San Francisco.

On the fifth day of January, Cassady's letter was addressed to both Jack and Joan, again riddling the opening of the first page with an impressive stream of verbal word-slinging: "Unfold the blasted blanket, unhinge the bloody gates; disperse the billowed drifts, make bellows blow piled coals, pour laden ladles, launch leviathans, roaring ranges rake the pale paste of pallid pals, dispelled in Eastern gloom, nullified is accursed weather, belittled is frostbitten feet, frozen fingers, frigid face, chilbrained children of chance, cripples caste [. . .]" It continues for eighty more words in the paragraph, a spontaneous stream of alliteration synthesizing Melville and Shakespeare into pure Keroassady poetry. Cassady chided Kerouac for his joblessness (though he was still working for Twentieth-Century Fox), urging him to suck it up and take on an eight-hour manual-labor job. In order to make the trip west, Kerouac had to rake up $150 minimum. Cassady had bought a 1941 Packard Coupe for Carolyn to cart her children around town. He promised to reach Lowell at last with Kerouac (as well as Denver to free his father from the slammer).

Carolyn read the letter after Cassady wrote it and reminded him to add the "most important part." Lately, a crackdown on narcotics in San Francisco had made it especially difficult to buy any marijuana on the street. Local dealers with an arrest record were suspected first, and others on the fringe became intimidated and soon backed off as well. The streets had dried up. Desperate, Cassady made it one of his express missions to go to New York and obtain pot. On January 10, he left.

Carolyn's attitude about Cassady's extended absences had mellowed a bit. She perhaps realized that there was no sense in attempting to tame the tiger. He always came back to her in the end. The day after he left, she mailed him a letter describing her sadness at watching his silhouette in contrast to the light of the train. Diana Hansen was still calling the house looking for child support, but Carolyn refused the collect-call charges, on the grounds that whatever she had to say (she needed a crib for the baby) could be accomplished with a twenty-one-cent stamp instead of a twenty-one-dollar phone call. Now that Carolyn had sensed a personal change in her husband, now that he seemed more responsible and less volatile, she liked having him around. His departure left her on "tenterhooks" concerning his personal safety. In the next letter she posted to him, only four days later, she revealed her suspicion that she was pregnant.

The day she wrote to Cassady, he was already in New Orleans, penciling back to her a postcard of the Huey P. Long

Bridge in Jefferson Parish, Louisiana. He was exhausted from the long train ride, used to completing his cross-country trips in half the time. The roundabout approach the steam engine took to reach its destinations, the long stops and even longer starts, made it seem more tedious than it really was. In Texas, there was snow; in Louisiana, rain. It was the same continental singsong that was by now second nature to him. On January 17, he had reached New York City.

CHAPTER EIGHT

IT IS WRITTEN

During Allen Ginsberg's stay at the psychiatric hospital, daily psychotherapy sparked his optimism that it would help him overcome his personal psychological issues (which weren't all that debilitating to start with). His father had written a letter to Lionel Trilling, expressing gratitude for his assistance in getting his son the help he needed and explaining the long history of Naomi's mental illness over the past twenty-five years. Louis Ginsberg believed that Allen's arrest had "shocked him into sobriety." With the Trilling's help Allen was capable of accomplishing great things in his lifetime.

Allen had developed a friendship with Carl Solomon, who was around the same age, of Jewish extraction, homosexual, and an intellectual. Unlike Ginsberg, Solomon had committed himself after he contemplated suicide. Solomon believed that the psychotherapy that he and Ginsberg received did nothing toward understanding their thoughts and feelings. The doctors were content as long as their behavior was overtly socially acceptable.

Excited about his new companion, Ginsberg wrote to Kerouac detailing Solomon's quirks and intellectual witticisms. Even at their first meeting, Ginsberg had sensed a shared affinity for mysticism and Surrealist literature, so much so that he was tempted to share his mystical Blakean experiences. However, Solomon retorted that what Ginsberg experienced wasn't all that unusual in a madhouse.

Still, Ginsberg was torn in half, as Kerouac was torn between taking care of his mother and going it alone in his harsh, misunderstanding world. Ginsberg felt that conformity "dulled" his mind and he harbored an innate fear of complying with society's norms. In his own "willful dark forebodings" lay an eternity that transcended "fact and truth" over the mazes that society ran people through. Ginsberg was aware of his unconscious rejection of "bourgeois standards," and that in order to be fully open to his psychotherapy, he would have to set aside his "loyalty and love" forever directed to the past.

His sole escape was cloaked in constant rivers of poetry

and journal writing, some drawn from the dreams he had of the Shrouded Stranger, of Lucien Carr as a "ball of flesh," or of lying under a blanket of cinders on some railroad tracks. Or of eternity and Heaven; that the "work of this world is the work of Heaven"; that the "love of this world is the love of Heaven." Introspection bordered on the edge of self-destruction only to be yanked back into a "living reality." Unlike Kerouac and Cassady, Ginsberg was resigned to knowing himself and, in the process, recording his findings in poetry. Poetry was an action that served a purpose similar to driving along empty highways for Kerouac and Cassady. But he did not need to travel, to drift along the continent in search of the unobtainable "It." His could be done looking out of his Paterson window, or in his room at the hospital, or tapped from the lingering remnants of a dream.

He directed much of his actions into long, studious expositions of Cézanne and Dante, in an effort to "fix" his mind. If he harbored "empty thoughts," he felt as if he were nothing more than a "zombie" searching for fulfillment. Furthermore, he had made it a point to write without resorting to Benzedrine. Having to *see* what he wanted to write before actually doing so was the key to meaningful work.

Ginsberg's dependence on Cassady had somewhat vanished, leaving only an empathetic longing to be with Cassady. In an effort to escape his desire for men, Ginsberg began dating a woman, with whom he was sexually active. But this turned out to be a failure. To Cassady, Ginsberg wrote in the summer of 1950 that she was spiteful toward him and that the only way he could relate to her at all was through conscious indifference.

Cassady, overwhelmed by his own personal problems, did not write back. On October 31, 1950, a frustrated Ginsberg wrote him another letter, this time relaying the circumstances leading up to the death of Bill Cannastra as well as a fragment of a new poem, "In Judgement." He also said that his attempts at fitting into society and its bourgeois values was failing. At his job, a couple of "nasty cunts" put the freeze on him, thoroughly illustrating the point to that end.

The following month, Cassady responded that he was broke and that his attempts at writing with his tape recorder had also proven to be a failure. He was concerned about the instability of railroad work and that his color-blindness could trip him up in the mandatory eye tests the railroad conducted. In the ensuing weeks, his letters to Ginsberg became seething with self-loathing and desperation. Cassady explained that he was reduced to eating only every twelve hours, sleeping every twenty; every eight hours was masturbation time. Sitting on the train as it rolled along the tracks, with his shaven head and maniacal stare, he passed his work hours staring straight ahead at the passing countryside without having any thoughts at all.

Furthermore, Cassady could not see the attraction his "Joan Anderson" letter held for Ginsberg and Kerouac, feeling that his writing was inadequate despite the three consecutive afternoons he had spent composing it. Their belief that the letter should be published fell on deaf ears. Hardly having the time to even correspond anymore, Cassady's desire to write began to dry up. His faith in his accomplishments was poorly conceived.

Ginsberg responded that Cassady was underestimating himself. After talking with Kerouac about the letter, his suggestion was that Cassady "blow faster" if he allowed himself to "skip around and write" whatever he felt. It was advice Kerouac began following himself. Ever the advocate for his close friends, Ginsberg could see quite correctly what they needed to improve in their writing even if he didn't know what to do with his own. Only after Kerouac pointed out that Ginsberg's best poems were those raw vestiges of poetic thought scribbled into his journal could he break free. He had to lift them intact, as poems of their own, and when he did, he found the liberation of his poetic voice.

THE MOTHEATEN OVERCOAT

After Cassady arrived in New York City, he went up the Hudson to Tarrytown, New York, where Diana and his son were living. Over the course of two days and nights, he felt that he had completely resolved any ongoing issues that she might have had about him and the support of their child. Satisfied that everything was okay, he returned to the city to see Ginsberg and Kerouac. He was also interested in reading

Holmes's new novel, aware of his appearance in *Go* as Hart Kennedy (in the section in New York in early 1949).

Arriving in Richmond Hill, a near-frozen Cassady discovered that Kerouac had momentarily gone out, but Joan welcomed him into the house by immediately handing him a beer and some hot water to soak his aching feet. Joan was entranced by Cassady's presence, by his excited and eager demeanor and that he was privy to a side of her husband that she had yet to see for herself. She was accustomed to moody Kerouac, pensive Kerouac, to self-absorbed, selfish, well-read Kerouac who always talked about Cassady but never really explained his homoerotic attraction. She sensed that Cassady was able to process life on many levels without keeping track of any. He could deliver references to philosophy, geography, snatches of poetry, as well as astute commentaries on society. This, she revealed later in her memoir, made her feel intellectually inferior.

However impressed she was, she did not feel the physical attraction for him that had ensnared a bevy of other women. His aggressive manner implied to her that he wanted to engage in a threesome with her and Kerouac, who did not show any signs that he would refuse such a suggestion. In fact, Kerouac felt that Cassady could teach them a thing or two about sex (and he secretly felt that Joan was sometimes frigid in bed). She wasn't willing to take on Cassady as a sexual mentor; however, she did give half-hearted permission for him to seek out a girl who would be willing. During the course of their marriage, it was her belief that she was catering to two men: a serious, neck-tied Kerouac of *The Town and the City*'s book jacket photo, and the open-collared tousle-haired Kerouac ruddy from whiskey and sheer physicality.

The last day that Cassady saw Kerouac in New York that year was on the way to a Duke Ellington concert with Henri Cru and Joan. Cru did not like Cassady and refused to give him a ride in his warm car. Cru was concerned about being embarrassed by Cassady's reckless actions. With Cassady, there was always a threat of losing something. It could be your woman, your dignity, your car, your wallet, or even yourself. That night the streets of Manhattan were frigidly cold and Joan, feeling bad for Cassady, asked Cru why he could not join them. To her, Cassady was a breath of fresh air and spontaneity, something sorely lacking in Kerouac's sober reserve. Cru remained firm. So, with that decision, Kerouac saw the last of Cassady as he walked away in his overcoat "bought specifically for the freezing temperatures of the east," as he wrote in the closing sentences of *On the Road*. Kerouac would have accompanied him if he hadn't been married. Instead, he sat in the idling car as Cassady headed for the train station.

THE SCROLL

On April 2, 1951, Kerouac took eight sheets of drawing paper and Scotch-taped them together, end to end, creating one continuous roll that he could feed into his typewriter. He was twenty-nine years old as of March. Perhaps following Allen Ginsberg's vow to desist from taking Benzedrine for his serious writing, Kerouac instead drank numerous cups of black coffee brewed by his wife. He began matter-of-factly, picturing himself telling Joan stories of Neal Cassady and the road: "I first met met Neal not long after my father died . . . I had just gotten over a serious illness that I won't bother to talk about." To simplify the task at hand, he used real names and consulted his notebooks, letters, and a "Self-Instruction" list to ensure accuracy. Though the novel stretched over the papers in a single paragraph, it maintained conventional punctuation. The thoughts outpaced the words being typed. Themes spewed forth: Life is a mystery; Mortality, bitten in the heels by the vicious cur of death; the veritable Shrouded Stranger forever finding your frantic steps; the interior quest, using an externalized setting with an extroverted character personified by Neal Cassady. If the road is a life lesson, then life is a road lesson, learned on a shimmering blacktop highway where the hope of what is to come is as elusive as Werner Herzog's desert mirages in *Fata Morgana*.

He wrote for hours. Referring to his journals and some details from Cassady's letters as well as some character sketches he had already created, he knew in advance exactly how his book would turn out. Kerouac also centered the chapters upon each stage of a road trip. This preparation destroys the myth that the composition of the novel was entirely spontaneous. In principal, it was just as planned as *The Town and the City*, the only difference being that Kerouac takes a more unorthodox approach to his prose, finding his own voice instead of using Thomas Wolfe's. Fueled by inspiration and an adept athlete at typing, he needed only the mental and physical exertion to endure such discipline. Ten days in, he wrote Ed White that he had accumulated about 86,000 words so far. He was tremendously exhilarated: "I don't know the date nor care and life is a bowl of pretty juicy cherries that I want one by one biting first with my cherry stained teeth."

By April 22, Kerouac had completed a novel approximately 125,000 words in length. He was rejuvenated at completing what he had struggled with for the last five and a half years. Writing to Cassady, he described *On the Road* as a novel about "you and me and the road." Ginsberg, who had read from the scroll as it peeled out of Kerouac's typewriter, told Cassady that the "hero is you." Roughly three weeks later, the scroll had reached a length of 120 feet and was finished.

FIRST IMPRESSIONS

Kerouac's first impulse was to show the novel to somebody he trusted for some objective feedback. John Clellon Holmes was just the person and therefore became the first to read the scroll in its entirety. On April 27, Kerouac handed the rolled-up novel to Holmes and waited for his response.

Holmes was first impressed by Kerouac's lack of conventional structure, which enabled him to capture a deluge of thoughts and impressions and thereby convey the immediacy of the novel. He wrote in his journal:

> I read Jack's book a few days ago. He wrote it in twenty days, and it is one long strip of tracing paper, one hundred and twenty feet long, it seems. It has much wonderful material in it. And, surprisingly enough, the style is straightforward, genuine, simple, still as lyric, but not as curlicue as it once was. If anything this book is, in its most important aspects, more mature than *The Town and the City.* It needs work. The transitions are weak. There is, perhaps, too much of it. The character of Neal, around which it gradually centers itself, needs to be focused a little more clearly. Those sections where he does not appear might be thinned out, pointed in his direction. It comes close to being a developed study of Neal, with his gradual changes from energetic juvenile delinquent to the kind of W. C. Fieldsian wanderer that Jack feels he is. The love in the book is charged and clear and masculine and good. . . . Jack's knowledge of this subject speaks for itself from every line. . . . [W]ith the necessary work, it will make a very exciting and important book indeed. All the material is here, it only needs to be sharpened, brought out, smoothed a bit.

Holmes felt that this time out, there would be no Wolfean comparisons, that Kerouac stylistically stood out from the rest and could now be considered a formidable presence on the contemporary literary scene.

However, the novel lacked an ending truly satisfying to Kerouac. Allen Ginsberg suggested that Neal Cassady provide one for him. Cassady's idea was that his character should end up as an "ulcerated old color-blind RR conductor who never writes anything good and dies a painful lingering death from postate [*sic*] gland trouble (cancer from excessive masturbation) at 45." Ultimately, he would be sent to San Quentin Prison for raping a teenaged girl.

Cassady was less than impressed by Kerouac's newest literary offering. He felt that Kerouac either had to forget the novel or make it broader in scope so that it spawned books, thereby making something comparable to Proust's *Remembrance of Things Past*. "I think he would profit," he wrote to Ginsberg, "by starting a book with the recollections of his early life as they were sent to me and then blend that into his prophetic DR. SAX. Of course, I'm sure I don't know what I'm talking about, but I do worry for him and want him happy." Cassady, however, did know what he was talking about. Kerouac had had such an idea in mind years before when he conceived of his autobiographical opuses as the Duluoz Legend; eventually, all of them would comprise the published novels *The Town and the City, Maggie Cassidy, Vanity of Duluoz,* and the road works.

When Kerouac learned of Ginsberg's letters to Cassady concerning his novel, he immediately wrote to Cassady. Kerouac was hypersensitive to his criticizing a book he had not read, lest he should misunderstand Ginsberg's description of it. What Ginsberg should have conveyed was that his portrait of Cassady was invigorated by life, love, boundless energy, and greatness. However, Cassady felt that Kerouac's use of him as the centerpiece of the novel was too "trivial."

On April 27, 1951, John Clellon Holmes brought the manuscript back to Kerouac and conveyed his first impressions. The one thing Holmes could not be was objective; he was much too familiar with the subject matter, not to mention being part of it. At the very least, he had also seen some of the earlier versions of *On the Road* and could at least mark its creative progress. Eagerly, he took Jack away from his apartment and walked with him all the way to a bar on the waterfront. It was evening and the cool rush of spring perfumed the city. Water lapped the pilings as Holmes exclaimed his keen admiration, that, with some further work, the book would make "exciting and stimulating" reading. Kerouac was happy, beaming. He told Holmes that together their books would "constitute a new trend in American literature!" Holmes's response to this was simple.

"Amen."

REJECTION

Kerouac moved his few belongings into Lucien Carr's loft. Joan, upset at the latest turn of events that had begun during *On the Road*'s spurious typing spree, had evicted him out of the apartment: Kerouac's libido was stimulated often by the subject matter he was typing, or so thought Joan when she glanced at a page and saw a passage about Bea Franco, the Mexican girl in Southern California he had picked up on a bus in September 1947. Around the desk, Kerouac had placed a screen so that he could type while Joan slept. From behind it he came to the bed in his bathrobe. "Quick!" he told her and he slipped between the covers with her.

By June, she knew that she was pregnant. However, Kerouac expressed his doubts that the baby was his, suggesting that maybe it was a dishwasher at a restaurant she worked in (after he moved out and came over one time he saw the young man in the apartment with her). Joan's insistence that the man was only a friend made no difference. Kerouace was paranoid and easily piqued into fits of jealousy. Insulted at his insensitivity and cruelty toward her, she kicked him out. The little fissure split into a widened gap. On June 10 Kerouac wrote Cassady: "Now I sit here, with sore phlebitis foot, my book finished, handed in, waiting for word from Giroux, a book about you and me, I sit here, my wife's not here, she's at her mother's, presumably tomorrow I move out and we part, I don't know what to do, where to go, on June 20 I may have a thousand dollars or more, meanwhile I stay with Lucien and Allen in loft."

THE FORGING OF *ON THE ROAD*

Kerouac took the scroll to the office of Robert Giroux at Harcourt, Brace. Giroux asked him what he had, and, with breathless delight Jack partially unrolled the scroll across the office floor, creating a long paper road.

"How the hell can the printer work from this?" Giroux wondered out loud.

Kerouac became angry. He rolled it back up, thrust it under his arm and stormed out of the office. Giroux had not read even a word, though if he had, his reaction could have been the same. The cramped, single-spaced immense paragraph of description and the ebullient rush of poetic prose was intimidating at first glance. Back at Carr's apartment, on May 22, Kerouac retyped the scroll into a more conventional typescript. A ream of typewriter paper piled up as he stopped every few minutes to unroll a bit more and continue typing. Kerouac sent it back to Harcourt, Brace, where it was immediately rejected.

Holmes volunteered his agent, Rae Everitt (the woman Kerouac had tried to hit on a few years back). Her first suggestion was to change its form, to reshape the work so that it was more approachable and less daunting to editors, who weren't altogether open to novel ideas and literary breakthroughs, but hoped only to squeeze out a buck riding on the back of established trends and genres. Kerouac had come too far to back down—what he had written was his masterwork. To rewrite the book, to reshape it into another *Town and the City,* would be taking several steps backward stylistically. Besides, *that* style hadn't sold in the numbers he had hoped. His instinct was to follow a new path and forget about any audience but himself.

As if in spite, he began to write even more unconventional prose. This time he did it in the form of "sketching," writing down immediate impressions of the sights before his eyes, confined to the length of a single notebook usually peeking out from his shirt pocket. It was a "prose description of a scene before the eyes. Ideally, for a *Book of Sketches,* one small page (of notebook size) about 100 words, so as not to ramble too much, and give an arbitrary form." It was an experimental writing technique lending itself easily to his emerging spontaneous prose style. By absorbing mundane commonalities and shedding new light upon them, he was seeing them with the vision of a true artist. Unconventional, and driven only by what his gut told him was right, Kerouac blazed through the pages of his pocket notebooks. The notebook sketching would be used to its greatest extent when he applied it to Cassady in *Visions of Cody.* Unlike *On the Road, Visions of Cody* was a detailed character study, not just of Neal Cassady, but of New York City, of cathedrals and diners, primping women, hungry minstrel-looking bums, masturbation on toilets, puke-stained sidewalks, and rank weeds growing between sidewalk cracks. It was to be an "enormous paean which would unite my vision of America with words spilled out in the modern spontaneous method," a "metaphysical study" of Cassady and America. In 1952, he began a series of fifteen notebooks of sketches as well, many of them taken while on the road during the ensuing years between 1952 up until 1957, before retyping them all into single a manuscript. It, like *Visions of Cody,* was published posthumously.

From 1952 to 1957, Kerouac also continued traveling the country and Mexico, writing prose pieces and poetry while shopping *On the Road* to publishers, all of which flatly rejected the novel. These were years of dejection for him despite the onrush of prose and poetry that still flowed from him with seemingly effortless ease. Working on *Visions of Cody,* he traveled across the country to take advantage of Cassady's offer of using his attic to write in. Kerouac lived with the Cassadys through the winter and into the spring of 1952. Thereafter, it was an endless string of addresses.

By August 7, 1955, Jack Kerouac was desperate and prone to drink. What he did not know was that Viking was circulating his manuscript in house. One of the editors, Evelyn Levine, was attracted by the male characterizations and the search for personal identity in the novel. Unlike the "Lost Generation," she opined, "his heroes stay right here [in America]—and try to find themselves." She did find the female characterizations troubling, however, as they were far less defined and served almost as window-dressing for the novel. Nonetheless, she was certain that the novel would be published eventually. Kerouac had in him honesty, perhaps even more refreshing and revealing than Saul Bellow, whom she felt was just a "jived-up Walt Whitman." The novel should come out at any cost even if it meant being a "literary and financial failure."

Shortly thereafter Kerouac's agent, Sterling Lord, sold an excerpt from *On the Road*, "The Mexican Girl," to the *Paris Review* for $50. This section of the manuscript dealt with Kerouac's romance with Bea Franco in Southern California in 1947. He was now known in New York City in literary circles and had caught the attention early on of noted editor Malcolm Cowley at Viking. Cowley saw that Kerouac had a great ability to tell stories earnestly and with real conviction. Cowley told him that *On the Road* had only been stalled from going further at Viking because of the threat of libel suits from the real-life characters, whose names remained in the typescript submitted to the editors. Kerouac still felt that the people would not object and vowed to get the required letters from the people in question. If he could not get permission, he would change those names. He also planned on switching some of the locales to further obscure fact from fiction.

By the fall of 1956, Kerouac waited anxiously for news from Viking about the novel's status. The publisher had been sitting on its decision for months now and he was running out of patience. He could have sold the novel as a cheap paperback just to get it out faster and generate some much-needed income. But the novel was somewhere within the slow turtle crawl of Viking's editorial process. Though Cowley showed interest in two other novels of Kerouac's as well (*Maggie Cassidy* and *Doctor Sax*), which he wanted to merge into one unified work, Kerouac felt that they were too different stylistically and wouldn't work (despite potential earnings of $40,000). He was now unyielding about changing anything he wrote just to please editors who had weaker visionary powers than he would have liked: "I've been through every conceivable disgrace now and no rejection or acceptance by publishers can alter that awful final feeling of death-of-life-which-is-death."

After some concessions, Viking made its offer and began making the book into a marketable commodity. Kerouac considered Viking editor Keith Jennison's inquiry whether he had any special "demands" regarding *On the Road*'s publication. Kerouac's wish was to keep the original title, feeling that it conveyed the novel's "picaresque" tone. *On the Road,* furthermore, was the "definite road of beatness." Skimming through the typescript at Malcolm Cowley's request, Kerouac had to look for other "unpraiseworthy libelous touches." At last the novel was going somewhere and Kerouac was eager to follow.

A March 22, 1957, interoffice memo affirmed that *On the*

Road was free of libel, and Viking readied it for printing with a slated publication month of September 1957. A manuscript acceptance report was passed out on April 4, 1957, summarizing the novel for the sales and marketing team. The sales pitch alerted them that the book was a "narrative of life among the wild bohemians." The book, Viking explained, told readers the story of the "beat generation":

> It carries us from New York to Denver, from Denver to San Francisco, then back to New York (with a detour through the Mexican settlements of the Central Valley)—then New York, New Orleans, San Francisco, Denver again, Chicago in seventeen hours in a borrowed Cadillac, Detroit, New York, Denver once more, and a Mexican town—the characters are always on wheels. They buy cars and wreck them, steal cars and leave them standing in fields, undertake to drive cars from one city to another, sharing the gas; then for variety they go hitch-hiking or sometimes ride a bus. In cities they go on wild parties or sit in joints listening to hot trumpets. They seem a little like machines themselves, machines gone haywire, always wound to the last pitch, always nervously moving, drinking, making love, with hardly any emotions except a determination to say "Yes" to any new experience. The writing at its best is deeply felt, and extremely moving. Again at its best this book is a

> celebration of the American scene in the manner of a latter-day Wolfe or Sandburg. The story itself has a steady, fast, unflagging movement that carries the reader along with it, always into new towns and madder adventures, and with only one tender interlude, that of the Mexican girl. It is real, honest, fascinating, everything for kicks, the voice of a new age.

A trip to Tangier to visit William Burroughs, who had left Mexico after fatally shooting his common-law wife in the head with his revolver, preempted any activity to move *On the Road* closer to publication. As Kerouac retyped Burroughs's scattered manuscript into a neat, tidy typescript titled *Naked Lunch,* the content of the work began to seep into his subconscious. He dreamed "of pulling endless bolognas from my mouth, from my very entrails, feet of it, pulling and pulling out all the horror of what Bull [Burroughs] saw, and wrote." But that was the effect Burroughs wanted, a sort of word exorcism in which he was "shitting out my educated Middlewest for once and for all." Burroughs's approach was quite opposite of Kerouac's, who still expressed modesty around his writing. "It's a matter of catharsis where I say the most horrible dirty slimy awful niggardliest posture possible—By the time I finish this book I'll be as pure as an angel, my dear." After several weeks with Burroughs, Kerouac tired of the squalid conditions and poverty of Tangier. Besides, *On the Road*'s publication was drawing near and he wanted to be in New York City for any last-minute work required to publicize the book.

AMERICA IN 1957

It was the year of modern consumer conveniences: Velcro was first manufactured, as was the new crystal powder breakfast drink from General Foods Corporation called Tang. Eveready manufactured "AA" sized batteries for the transistor radios that were all the rage with America's teenagers. Shoppers could buy frozen pizza in the frozen food section and the introduction of the fine cuisine of microwave cooking in *Better Homes and Gardens* magazine.

American culture was transforming as fast as televisions were being sold, with 47,200,000 sets sitting in 39,500,000 homes across the nation. What was there to watch back then? For the kids there was *The Mickey Mouse Club, Lassie, Leave it to Beaver, The Lone Ranger, Sea Hunt, The Adventures of Robin Hood,* and *Circus Boy.* Dad could enjoy westerns like *Gunsmoke* and *Have Gun Will Travel, Wagon Train, The Life and Legend of Wyatt Earp,* and *Cheyenne.* There was police drama, such as *Dragnet,* and courtroom drama, such as *Perry Mason.* Mom had her pick of comedy and musical hours: *The Loretta Young Show, Our Miss Brooks, Bachelor Father,* and *The Adventures of Ozzie and Harriet.* Soap manufacturers such as Procter and Gamble, Colgate-Palmolive and Pepsodent still sponsored afternoon soap operas that had successfully transformed themselves from radio serials to daytime weekly broadcasts. The 1957 film *Peyton Place* helped transform the genre into hundreds of spin-offs, putting a new twist on the safe roles of wives and mothers who seemed to be doing nothing but dusting furniture and baking pies while the rest of the family was at school and work.

In sports, Jackie Robinson announced his retirement and the fourteen-year-old Bobby Fischer became the newest and most unlikely chess champion. In film, there was an amazing spectacle of new color films intermixed with the decline of black-and-white features in movie theaters: *The Bridge on the River Kwai,* Stanley Kubrick's *Paths of Glory,* Elvis Presley's *Jailhouse Rock, Sweet Smell of Success, The Three Faces of Eve, 12 Angry Men, Witness for the Prosecution,* and *Gunfight at the O.K. Corral* (again, courtroom dramas and westerns), and Marlon Brando's dashing handsome looks brightened up the otherwise bleak Korean War drama *Sayonara.* The spirit of James Dean still lingered in film culture despite his death in 1955. He embodied teen angst and brought to the streets the residual frustration of stuffy living rooms and the niceties of formal parlors. It was the disaffection of youth too young to be in the Second World War, but old enough to know the memories of their fathers. Dean's two feature films of 1955, a film version of John Steinbeck's *East of Eden* and *Rebel Without a Cause,* planted the Dean image into America's teenaged youth consciousness. Dean's portrayal of the troubled Nick Ray was a pale forerunner of the then-unknown

Dean Moriarty, and the real-life Dean's sexual interests extended to both men and women. Did the success of the film lead Kerouac (who had invented names for the characters for *On the Road*) to jump on James *Dean*'s bandwagon by using his last name and *Sal* Mineo's first to cement the relevance of the novel into adolescent pop consciousness? Dean's death in a car wreck added a dangerous edge to the automobile, now no longer merely viewed as a vehicle for the family's Sunday drives.

Literature had its moments as well: Dr. Seuss took his slice at the popular *Dick and Jane* series with his absurdity *The Cat in the Hat;* the Eliot Ness drama *The Untouchables;* Mary McCarthy's embellished autobiography, *Memories of a Catholic Girlhood;* Alan Fleming's new books, *The Diamond Smugglers* and *From Russia with Love.* However, there was nothing even remotely like Jack Kerouac's *On the Road.* His was a brand-new take on post–World War II America's sordid underbelly; GIs adrift on railroad tracks and lonely highways; jazz tempos simmering in a marijuana haze; wet bar napkins and filled ashtrays. There were women dispensing with the notion of "saving themselves" for marriage and sometimes, like men, functioning at a purely physical level. The jazz masters laid out their temporal visions to the soundtrack of horns and the abstract shuffling of backbeats, striving to push above and beyond, as Kerouac did, the parameters of chordal structure. Coltrane released the formidable *Blue Train,* foreshadowing the carefully controlled musical intensity that flowered fully in his next LP, *Giant Steps* (1959). In that same year, Miles Davis released his groundbreaking *Kind of Blue*.

And there was rock'n'roll.

Elvis Presley's final appearance on the *Ed Sullivan Show* heightened the hysteria over the charismatic singer and his hit song that year, "All Shook Up." Presley's fame and wealth allowed him to buy a mansion in the heart of American country and western music, Memphis, Tennessee. He called it Graceland. There were Bill Haley and His Comets, Fats Domino's "Blueberry Hill," Buddy Holly's "Everyday," Jerry Lee Lewis's "Great Balls of Fire." New careers were also taking off for other singers such as Patsy Cline in country and western, and the great soul singer Jerry Butler.

So influential and pervasive was the new music scene that Kerouac wrote to Sterling Lord suggesting a new title for *On the Road*: "It occurred to me, maybe it would double the sales to change the title to *Rock and Roll Road* or at least to invent a similar subtitle."The idea was nixed by all parties concerned.

America, was again reinventing itself, redefining what it was and what it stood for. Beneath the facade of gentility rebels stirred, amassing their strength in the name of freedom of expression. Artists shrugged away the label of modernity in favor of another mode of expression peculiar to their generation; the postmodernists were here.

IN THE LION'S DEN

When Kerouac was staying at the Hotel Mouniria in Tangier, he had written to his agent asking him to begin selling his more experimental writing. The irony of that year of 1957, when his luck changed for once, and he became known for the lyrical *On the Road,* was that he had moved on stylistically. The re-edited *On the Road* in its soon-to-be-published form was a closer cousin to *The Town and the City* than was the latest crop of writings that Lord was shopping around the city. There was his Buddhist tome *Some of the Dharma,* along with *Visions of Cody,* the novella *Tristessa* (about his relationship with the Mexican Indian girl Esperanza Villanueva), *The Subterraneans,* and a collection of blues poems *Book of Blues.* His prose now resembled what he described as a "series of rhythmic expostulations of speech." His unorthodox grammatical structure and spontaneous flowing of words was guaranteed to alienate skittish publishers. As with other American writers who stuck to their stylistic guns (like Hemingway and Faulkner), Kerouac's work was never an easy sell until after the success of *On the Road.*

Fearing that Kerouac would tamper with already perfected copyedits and proofing, Viking never sent the author any galleys of the book. He wrote to Malcolm Cowley from Berkeley, California, wondering where they were. Shortly thereafter, Sterling Lord informed Kerouac that the review copies of *On the Road* were printed and were sent out to reviewers. In July 1957, Kerouac had his own advance copies delivered in a sealed box.

The Berkeley cottage was occupied at the time by Kerouac, Cassady, LuAnne Henderson, and Al Hinkle, all prominent characters in *On the Road*. Their respective pseudonyms only thinly disguised each. The first copy was handed to Neal, the hero of the novel, who held between its covers the instrument of his own early demise. The book would also change Kerouac's life and become, as for Cassady, one of the contributing factors to his premature death less than twelve years later. The book acted as an instant aphrodisiac for LuAnne Henderson, who sought to sleep with Kerouac for the rest of the night (though he claimed to Ginsberg that he declined the offer).

Before leaving California, Kerouac gave an interview to the *San Francisco Examiner*. He portrayed himself as a phenomenon, making it appear that his forthcoming work was written without thought or pretense over a period of three weeks. "I write about ten feet in a good day," he told the interviewer, "I never edit. Whatever you try to delete from a manuscript, that's what is most interesting to a doctor." He took time to explain his background, that he came from Lowell born to working-class French Canadian parents, of getting "tired" of the academic life at Columbia University and quitting to join the Merchant Marines and that he had also married twice. He spoke of his love for Wolfe, Proust, and Joyce: "I'm not interested in their methods, only in their concerns. Joyce was interested in language, Proust in memory. I'm interested in both." To further bind his intentions for his life, he made public his plan to continue writing "the story of my life." "When I'm through you'll have the whole thing on one shelf. That's the grand scheme."

Kerouac was in Orlando, Florida, with his mother during the latter part of the summer of 1957. Knowing that his book was coming out shortly, he returned to New York City on September 2 and stayed with a friend, Joyce Glassman. Together they went to Donnelly's Bar with a copy of *The New York Times* and began rifling through the pages.

The reviewer for the *New York Times,* Charles Poore, enamored of Ernest Hemingway, John Steinbeck, and Bernard Malamud, among others, had passed on reviewing *On the Road* because of illness. Had he done so, the fate of the novel might have changed, dashing Kerouac's sophomore effort onto the rocks of literary failure. Such was Poore's clout that many publishers determined their publication dates based on who would write the book review that day (Poore's day was Thursday). This Thursday, Gilbert Millstein had filled in with a serious appraisal of *On the Road* as a cultural milestone:

"'On the Road' is the second novel by Jack Kerouac, and its publication is a historic occasion in so far as the exposure of an authentic work of art is of any great moment in an age in which the attention is fragmented and the sensibilities are blunted by the superlatives of fashion (multiplied by a millionfold by the speed and pound of communication)." The critic predicted that though the vast majority of book reviewers would misunderstand the intentions of its author and that the work would be misconstrued as superficial, the writing itself was the "most beautifully executed, the clearest, and the most important utterance yet made by the generation Kerouac himself named years ago as 'beat,' and whose principal avatar he is."

On that same day in Little Rock, Arkansas, the Little Rock Central High School became a vital battleground for the civil rights movement in America. Watching through the glass eye of television cameras, America was transfixed by the nine courageous African American students, under federal escort, attempting to enter an all-white school. The federal government had vowed to eliminate segregation in the public school system. Specifically, a little fifteen-year-old girl named Elizabeth Eckford stood by herself amid a growing crowd and told the press, "I tried to see a friendly face somewhere in the mob—someone who maybe would help. I looked into the face of an old woman and it seemed a kind face, but when I looked at her again, she spat on me."

The school board requested that the plan for desegregation be temporarily suspended. Immediately the motion was denied by the Federal District Court. President Eisenhower sent a telegram to the governor of Arkansas assuring that the "federal constitution will be upheld by me by every legal means at my command." When the Little Rock Nine finally entered the school, rioting broke out. Soon thereafter, the nine were taken out of the back of the school for their safety. A white student named Robin Woods said, "That was the first time I'd ever gone to school with a Negro, and it didn't hurt a bit."

It was a crowning moment of a new mentality toward minority races and *On the Road,* if anything, stirred the cultural pot further by making it okay to not only write about risky peccadilloes, but to empathize (if naively) with the racial plight of minorities. Though Little Rock's importance overshadowed Kerouac's accomplishments, his timing was right. He capitalized, by chance and not design, upon the consciousness of an America that either resisted or embraced its changes.

Kerouac woke up from a dream and characteristically pulled a piece of paper from his bedside and wrote it down: "I had a white bandage on my head from a wound, the police are after me around the dark stairs of wood near the Victory Theatre in Lowell, I sneak away—come to the boulevard where a parade of children chanting my name hide me from the searching police as I duck along their endless ranks keeping low."

Requests for interviews flooded the publicity office of Viking. Judging by the jacket photo of Kerouac and the sensational subject matter of the novel, he was already a hit with the press: young, handsome, dark, mysterious, and sensationally candid pitch about items considered taboo by others. Kerouac was sought after at a feverish pace; some went straight to him, who never could say "no" to anybody even if it was in his best interest to do so. He granted an interview to Maurice Dolbier of the *New York Herald Tribune* in which he shared his vision of *beat,* his novel *Doctor Sax,* and that the goal of his travels was "ecstasy." Dolbier saw that the scroll manuscript was being rolled up, that it took a long time, and that a cocker spaniel "behaving like an outraged reviewer" had chewed the end of it. Kerouac said that beatness was "part of a religious movement, the Second Religiousness that Oswald Spengler prophesied for the West." Dolbier wrote, "when one's mind begins to boggle at the vision of Presley's sideburns and Jean-Paul Sartre and Brando on a motorcycle as units in a religious revival, you are reminded of the posthumous adoration of James Dean and the trance-visions induced by drugs, and you wonder. Mr. Kerouac hammers out the case with anonymous instances of strange manifestations, foreshadowings of the end of the world and the Second Coming, hipsters who have seen angels and devils, and reports quite casually that he too has heard heavenly music while speeding along a California highway."

Not all of the critics were kind toward Kerouac. Though he had impressed the very top, the fallout from the rest would inflict more harm than good on the beleaguered writer. Herbert Gold's review in the *Nation* slammed Kerouac's credibility, attacking the writer and not the book itself. He was a "perennial bar mitzvah boy." Others claimed he was the "Neanderthal of the typewriter." Phoebe-Lou Adams criticized the "severe simplicity" of the writing and said that the novel "constantly promises a revelation or a conclusion of real importance and general applicability," but "cannot deliver any such conclusion because Dean is more convincing as an eccentric than as a representative of any segment of humanity."

In a valiant effort to appease the press, Kerouac continued to feel obligated to explain his beat philosophy to journalists who were more interested in his quirks than any spiritual insights that he could offer. The *Village Voice* was kinder, seeing in Kerouac a sort of long-lost wayward brother. They noted his appearance on John Wingate's television program *Nightbeat* in mid-September: "The author of 'On the Road' was on 'Nightbeat' last week (looking and sounding remarkably like the late James Dean, incidentally)." When Wingate asked him about the word *beat*, Kerouac's response was "I feel beat, do you?" He was, he told Wingate, "waiting for God to show his face." More important, the *Voice* was glowing about Kerouac's second novel: "People are already leafing curiously through it in bookstores, toting it around the Village, hugging it under their arm as they ride the subway to work . . . despite the complete and incomprehensible lack of publisher's advertising so far, the first printing sold out a week after publication." There was a good reason for the novel's overwhelming success during the first quarter of its sales, it was sensational and dared to utter what everybody else kept a secret. The *Village Voice* stated:

> Kerouac is not just a writer, not just a talent, but a *voice,* as Hemingway, Henry Miller, the early Gide were and are to those who are disposed to listen. Kerouac has taken the way he and his friends lived and felt about life in the years 1947-1950 and written a lusty, noisily lyrical, exuberantly overwritten book about it all. But more important than that, he offers a belief, a rallying point for the elusive spirit of the rebellions of these times, that silent scornful sit-down strike of the disaffiliated which has been the nearest thing to a real movement among the young since the end of World War II. "On the Road" is as crucial to the social history of the past 10 years in America as "The Lonely Crowd." (*Village Voice,* September 17, 1957)

The novel had made its mark, and its effect was evident upon artists on the fringe, who saw how empowering it was to be honest in one's work, even if there was a hefty price to pay. The sudden attention to his work after years of struggle and obscurity became overwhelming. Though he became the butt of jokes for lame dead-end comedians, Kerouac was respected among his peers, and he was an inspiration to writers such as Hunter S. Thompson, who felt a kinship with the awkward figure on the Wingate show. Fifty years after the novel's publication, the book continues to inspire and awe those who pick it up for the first time. For those who are seasoned readers of Kerouac, the book serves as a signpost to the past, marking a transition, a rite of passage when they first realized that there is a world out there beyond their hometowns where starlight shimmers in the desert heat and the wind blows lonesome snow drifts across mountain passes like cold, unfeeling fingers.

Bibliography

Burroughs, William. *The Letters of William Burroughs,* Volume I (Viking, 1994).

Charters, Ann. *Kerouac: A Biography* (St. Martin's Press, 1994).

Cassady, Carolyn. *Off the Road: My Years with Cassady, Kerouac, and Ginsberg* (Viking, 1991).

Cassady, Neal. *Collected Letters: 1944–1967* (Viking, 2005).

Cassady, Neal. *The First Third* (City Lights, 1971).

Christopher, Tom. *Neal Cassady, Volume I, 1926–1940* (1991).

Christopher, Tom. *Neal Cassady, Volume II, 1941–1946* (1991).

Ginsberg, Allen, and Neal Cassady. *As Ever: The Collected Correspondence of Allen Ginsberg and Neal Cassady* (Creative Arts Book Company, 1971).

Ginsberg, Allen. *Collected Poems: 1947–1997* (HarperCollins, 2006).

Ginsberg, Allen. *The Book of Martyrdom and Artifice: First Journals and Poems 1937–1952* (Viking, 2006).

Kerouac, Jack. *Atop an Underwood* (Viking, 2000).

Kerouac, Jack. *Book of Sketches* (Viking, 2006).

Kerouac, Jack. *On the Road* (Viking, 1957).

Kerouac, Jack. *Selected Letters I* (Viking, 1995).

Kerouac, Jack. *Visions of Cody* (Viking, 1993).

Kerouac, Jack. *Windblown World* (Viking, 2006).

Maher Jr., Paul. *Empty Phantoms* (Thunder's Mouth Press, 2005).

Maher Jr., Paul. *Kerouac: His Life and Work* (Taylor Trade, 2007).

McNally, Dennis. *Desolate Angel: Jack Kerouac, The Beat Generation and America* (DaCapo Press, 2003).

Morgan, Bill. *I Celebrate Myself: The Somewhat Private Life of Allen Ginsberg* (Viking, 2006).

Plummer, William. *The Holy Goof: A Biography of Neal Cassady* (Thunder's Mouth Press, 2004).

Sandison, David, and Graham Vickers. *Neal Cassady: The Fast Life of a Beat Hero* (Chicago Review Press, 2006).

Acknowledgments

The author extends thanks and appreciation to the curators of the archive of Jack Kerouac at New York Public Library–Berg Collection. Archival matter used for reference includes correspondence to and from Jack Kerouac and his associates, and the notebooks and journals of the author during his "On the Road" years stemming from 1945 to 1950. Appreciation is also given to John Sampas, literary executor to the Estate of Jack and Stella Kerouac, for his competent management and shrewd handling of Jack Kerouac's literary legacy.

Index